ONE YEAR OF RESEARCH ON ALM 2016

Serge MOULIN

ALM-VISION

All rights reserved. In application of French law of the 11th of March 1957 (article 41) and intellectual property law of the 1st of July, supplemented by law of the 3rd of January 1995, any partial or total copy of this publication for collective use is strictly forbidden without the express permission of the author. Every reproduction or use without the consent of the author is illegal.

©2016 S. MOULIN. ALM-VISION. All rights reserved.

ISBN 978-1-326-92472-0

One year of research on ALM: 2016

Table of contents

INTRODUCTION 5

PRICING of BONDS with Risk Premium: market value versus economic value 9

    A simple but very speaking example 10

    Mathematical formulation 12

    Ex ante provisioning 16

    Pricing of CDS and insurance guarantees 16

    Estimating the probability of default $h(t)$ and margin $\mu(t)$ 22

    Conclusion 25

SELLING A NON PERFORMING UNSECURED RETAIL LOANS BOOK: strategic considerations and methodology of pricing 27

    Valuation of Non Performing Loans 27

    Strategic motivations of a sale 33

MODELING and PRICING PREPAYMENTS: *a market approach* 39

    Introduction 39

    Elements influencing prepayments 40

    Modeling customer behavior 44

    Passage to the continuous model 57

    Pricing the option 65

    Conclusion 81

    References 82

PRICING REAL ESTATE, an elegant modeling 84
Pricing methodology used in the industry for commercial R.E. 85
    Pricing using a DDM methodology 87

    Time effect in Real Estate and stress scenarios 95

    Other elements to take into account in R.E. pricing 99

    Conclusion 101

    References 102

The NEW STANDARD for INTEREST RATE RISK in the BANKING BOOK defined by the BASEL COMMITTEE on Banking Supervision: Finally, ALM makes its revolution. 104
    Summary 104

    Presentation of the new regulation 105

    9 key principles for banks 106

    3 principles for supervisors 114

    The standardized framework 114

    Some general comments 118

    Conclusion 129

The NEW STANDARD for IRRBB: UNDERSTANDING the complementarity of approaches in estimating the variation in Economic Value of Equity (EVE) and the sensitivity of Net Interest Margin (NIM) – a CASE STUDY 130
    Introduction 130

    Static versus dynamic gaps 130

    A simple example 133

    Duration and modeling of the fixed rate loans book of a commercial bank 137

    Liabilities: focusing on the Non Maturity Deposits ("NMD") 145

    NIM simulation and effect of IR on the value of the bank 150

The static gap methodology is translating the concern of the regulator in case of liquidation. 156

Banks' ALM objective is to stabilize the NIM under the constraint of respecting the limits on variation in EVE. 158

The gap buckets analysis 162

Conclusion 164

Some qualitative macroeconomic and strategic perspectives on the current economic situation and what scenario we can imagine for 2017. 166
    Fundamental macroeconomic issues remain in Europe......................166

A multi-polar world is emerging with "Realpolitik" coming back challenging traditional political powers. 175

In this environment, a crisis scenario can arise at any time in Europe 176

About ALM-VISION...178
Disclaimer 179

INTRODUCTION

2016 has been a very special year for banks and insurance companies.

First, the industry had to cope with a very exceptional market environment. Indeed, Euro interest rates went into negative for duration below five years on swap and up to ten years for the best govies. In parallel, spreads decreased to levels not seen since 2007. Finally, the massive intervention of the European Central Bank (ECB) maintained real interest rates negative, with nominal interest rates systematically below an almost null inflation.

Investing in these conditions was a real challenge, as well as paying an attractive benefit participation to policy holders. Life insurance suffered, especially for companies with minimum guarantee rates. It faces a difficult future should the situation continue. In addition, life insurance tax haven status is always more challenged by governments who remain in a complex dialectic with the industry since this one was the first buyer of many of its government papers (helped by the Solvency II rules not applying a stress test to Euro-govies).

Meanwhile, bank margins were pushed under pressure as their funding costs are structurally caped and partially insensitive to interest rates (IR) whereas their loan books suffered from low interest rates, the massive prepayments waves and the subsequent fierce competition which pushed margins further down. With the latent no growth crisis generating Non Performing Loans (NPLs) in the balance sheet of many institutions, the state of banks remains heterogeneous, some being still weak whereas others are currently extremely well capitalized.

Both industries faced a massive regulatory wave: 2016 is the first year of implementation of Solvency II, an extremely complex reform, which still is not fully mastered from an Asset Liability Management (ALM) point of view by too many insurance companies. On their side, banks are struggling to cope with Basel III whereas a new fundamental regulation for ALM - IRRBB d368 - was released by the Basel Committee this past spring.

This small book gathers research articles that were published during 2016. All of them are related to the operational impact in terms of asset and liability modeling of the current situation. If some include theoretical views, these ones were developed because our decisions need to be based on rigorous and rational grounds.

- The first paper – pricing of bonds – explains how building of the price of risk is made by the market. It further addresses reasons why institutions should remain cautious when using Credit Default Swap (CDS) spread in reverse engineering since these ones include a massive risk premium in addition to the loss expectation.
- The second paper continues on the subject of risk by providing formalization for NPL valuation and strategy of sale. ALM-Vision has been active on this field this year and definitely the subject may require additional study, especially in order to formalize the policy of provisioning of institutions.
- The third paper covers a subject also linked to the current crisis: prepayments of fixed rate loans as well as valuation of lapse risk in life insurance contracts with minimum guaranteed rate. 2016 was touched by one of the most massive wave of prepayment in the industry ever. If the prepayment wave reduces in intensity with the "Noria" effect on the loan book, it remains a fundamental topic in ALM.
- The fourth paper seeks a formalization of the observed evolution of yields in Real Estate investment. The subject is important for insurance companies because the standard model under Solvency II is capital consuming. It is also important for direct investors because Real Estate appeared during this year as a safe haven. However, yields were also impacted by the decrease of IR. Finally, many investors discovered the risks that they face in symmetry of the banks, for the refunding of their investments. A rigorous strategy of refunding of Real Estate funds requires to both understand and model links between interest rates, rent indexes and yields.
- The fifth and sixth papers focus on IRRBB368. The new regulation is a revolution for ALM management and banks have one year only to implement it. But before being in a position to do so, they need to

understand what the regulation is about, what its goal is, what its benefits and constraints are.

- Finally, as we did at the end of our previous book, we get away from the quantitative approach to seek to analyze in a more entertaining qualitative manner the current macroeconomic and geostrategic environment and deduce from it which stress scenarios and which risks may be faced in 2017 with the purpose of discussing the fundamental issues underlying complex trends that we observe.

We all wish you our best for the next year and thank you for our exchanges and your support which are the first source of inspiration.

PRICING of BONDS with Risk Premium: market value versus economic value

During the crisis, prices of bonds reached levels which were difficult to explain by just using the formula heard everywhere at the time: "the market is repricing risk". Actually, some bonds saw their prices collapsing far beyond the worsening of the global economic climate and their specific situation. Clearly classical models weren't working anymore. We propose here a modeling inspired from insurance which remains valid even though the classical assumption of pure and perfect markets isn't valid anymore. This is actually the case most of the time on the bond market where liquidity is reduced both on offer and demand and risk takers requests a premium in addition of the best estimate of the risk.

The same approach applies to CDS and financial guarantees which prices can significantly differ from the cash market because both markets are compartmentalized and buyers of the same underlying risks (the insurers) aren't expecting the same return on their investment.

This methodology explains much better price building and opens space to distinguish market price from economic value, a key argument against the danger of the new tendency toward a "full marked to market" approach. This paper doesn't present any new scientific model but just focus on explaining simply some basic economic mechanisms of market actors which conduct to the creation of this risk margin.

There is an abundant literature about the "reduced-form models", which are criticized for underestimating the CDS spread. Actually, our simple analysis is conformed to this observation and conduct to rehabilitate these models. The fact that the CDS market developed strongly before the crisis with valuation of CDS at 0 at the time of execution doesn't mean that there isn't a risk premium in the product as there is one for bonds.

A simple but very speaking example

During the crisis, spreads on very long term utilities bonds, water companies in Western Europe jumped to more than 350 bp for the 50 years bonds.

Utilities companies, specially managing waters, are the owners of heavy networks which can't be replaced or put in concurrence on their area. Indeed recovery is extremely high because default can come only from a technical mismanagement inside the company (technical or financial accident). Out of these technical elements, a collapse of these companies is difficult to imagine: most European cities are more than 2000 years old and remained inhabited without interruption. Water consumption is the most basic necessity of human beings. Water utilities companies have insurance against catastrophic accidents. Their cash flow are extremely predictable and none was such badly financially exposed that the 2008 financial crisis put its balance sheet in danger. The utilities have always had rating between BBB and BBB+, actually the best possible notation from rating agencies, considering their activity and size of balance sheet. They are one of the most stable class of rating, which is a better predictor of their solidness than the rating itself.

The most likely explanation of the increase of their spreads, if the market was "repricing risk", would have been the risk of a jump of their unpaid bills. Still, this is correlated with the economic growth and with a recession below 5%, it was hard assuming a massive default of the European population in big cities (furthermore major cities often show better resilience to adverse economic conditions, due to the higher percentage of services and administrations).

Let assume recoveries of 80%, 60% and 40% and calculate the probability of survival after 50 years for a BBB+ utilities bond with a Z-spread of 50 bps before the crisis and of 350 bps during the crisis using the formula provided by assuming that the market doesn't request any risk premium (prices are "pure and perfect", there is an infinite number of buyers and sellers of the insurance with infinite access to funding so that the rate of return converges toward zero):

Probability of survival in 50 years		
LGD \ CDS	0.5%	3.5%
20%	29%	0.02%
40%	53%	1.3%
60%	66%	5%

Recoveries are usually very high with utilities and in this case, whatever the chosen recovery, one arrives to two conclusions:

- First, the variation in the probability of survival between the situation before the crisis and after appear way too high with an implied probability of default of a BBB+ bond which has been in this rating class for years and passed through the whole crisis with an unchanged rating above 95% over the next 50 years.
- Second, even before the crisis, this probability of default sounds pretty high.

The CDS market is showing the same pattern. United Utilities Water Ltd is UK's largest listed water company, it manages a vast network of wastewater in the North West of England, providing water to 7 million people. Its core business is strictly regulated. The activity is highly predictable in long term with revenues indexed on inflation and a significant long term debt. The company saw its operating profits slightly growing during the last five years and maintained its BBB+ rating while reinforcing its capital. Gearing is stable at 58% and average duration of the debt is over 25 years. Clearly the crisis had no significant impact on the company. Still its CDS jumped probably partly due to the risk of having UUW refunding its 6 Billions debt at a much higher spread. But notice that the IR decrease during the period reduced the absolute cost of debt. The move can't be subsequently attributed to the sole degradation of the risk of the company.

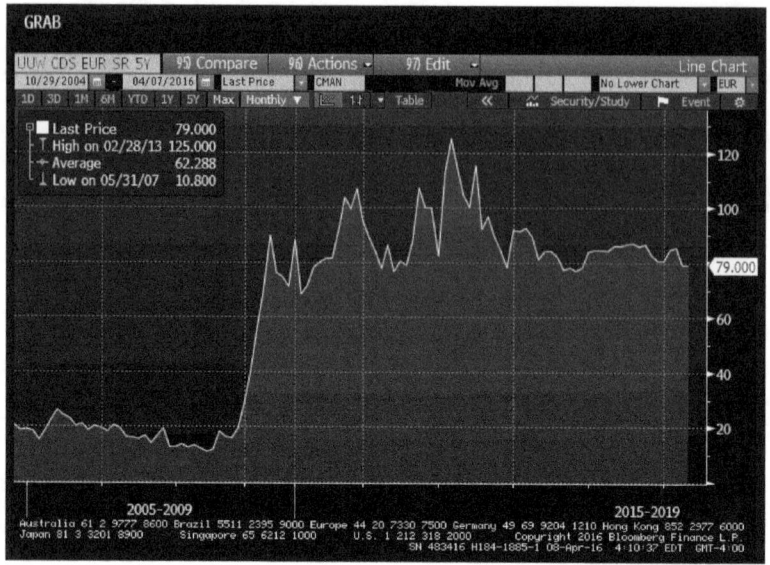

Of course, the prices weren't trading during the crisis and the z-spread had to be adjusted for a liquidity premium symmetrical to the one observed for the best ratings (the German Federal state basically) but still the result remain: **the movements in prices were not justified by any objective degradation of the risk of the names, whether idiosyncratic or coming from the market**. The so called "repricing of the risk" by the market was referring to something else.

Mathematical formulation

Let be τ the date of default of an issuer, let define the following two probabilities:

$q(t).dt = P\left[\tau \in [t, t+dt]\right]$ the probability of default between t and $t+dt$

$h(t).dt = P\left[\tau \in [t, t+dt] | \tau \geq t\right]$ the probability of default between t and $t+dt$ knowing that the issuer is still alive at t.

Classically, the survival function is $S_t = P[\tau \geq t]$, that is the probability that the default takes place after date t.

Assuming classically that evolutions are independent (future depends only on the present), one gets:

$$q(t).dt = S_t.h(t).dt$$

Which gives:

$$P(\tau \leq t) = 1 - S_t = \int_0^t q(s).ds = \int_0^t S_s.h(s).ds$$

thus $dS_t = -h(t).S_t.dt$ and $S_t = S_0.e^{-\int_0^t h(s).ds}$

- For a constant instantaneous default probability h(t)=h, one gets: $S_t = e^{-h.t}$, the survival function is decreasing exponential.
- For a constant instantaneous default probability per segment h(t)=h$_i$ pour $t \in [t_{i-1}, t_i]$, one gets: $S_t = S_{t_{i-1}}.e^{h_i.t}$

Price of zero-coupon must now take into account a possible default. Let write r the interest rate of the risk free 0-coupon expiring at t:

$$P(t) = E[e^{-r.t}] = e^{-r.t}$$

Note that this is a simple model with a defined fixed r. Note also that in realty such a bond doesn't exist.

When one assumes, in case of default, loss of 100% (let note LGD = 100% for Loss Given Default), the formula becomes with a risk premium μ(t) at time t:

$$P(t) = E\left[S_t.e^{-(r+\mu)t}\right] = e^{-(r+\mu+h).t}$$

The risk premium priced by the market depends on many elements:

- The uncertainty on the estimation of parameter h: the more difficult or uncertain the estimation is, the higher the requested risk premium,
- The demand for insurance (buyers of the CDS or seller of the bonds) and of offer (sell of CDS or purchase of the bond by the insurers or investors),
- The capacities of the insurers or investors: access to funding, cost of this funding. This is all the most relevant that there is margin calls in case of negative MtM,
- The capacity for insurers to diversify the risk between names,
- The profitability of other risks.

The classical theory imagines a "pure and perfect market" where there is an infinite number of buyers and sellers of insurance contracts with infinite capacities of refunding. These actors compete perfectly and the price finds its equilibrium with a risk premium equal to zero. Obviously, there isn't such a market, the reality is different. Indeed, there is no name where liquidity is such between sellers and buyers of protection so that the risk premium equals 0. Sometimes it can happen, sometimes, one even get negative risk premium (during flies to quality) but most of the time, it doesn't. The market finds a balance exactly as the insurance market never prices at the best estimate alone any insurance contract.

In reality, many of the assumptions of the classical theory are wrong:

- actors don't have access to risk free rate to refund themselves,
- actors have limited resources,
- actors can't fully diversified their portfolio,
- volumes are limited on CDS due to the small number of players,
- actors can't act without capital on the market. This capital must generate an excess return in proportion to the risk and in comparison to the other possibilities of return (like on the equity market...).

During the crisis, these limitations were just exacerbated since the number of players shrank as well as their resources and risk appetite. The risk premium increased in our example by 250 bp / 300 bp without any significant increase of the hazard rate h (h necessarily increased with the worsening of the economic situation but absolutely not in proportion). The price of the bonds collapsed without direct link to its true risk.

If LGD is no longer supposed equal to 100%, the general formula becomes:

$$P(t) = (1-LGD).\int_0^t e^{-(r+\mu).s}.h(s).S_s.ds + e^{-(r+\mu).t}.S_t$$

The first term expresses the recovery in case of default before expiration of the bond. The second term is the actualized value of the reimbursement at expiration in case of survival.

And for h(s) = h constant:

$$P(t) = (1-LGD).\frac{h}{r+\mu+h}.\left[1-e^{-(r+\mu+h).t}\right] + e^{-(r+\mu+h).t}$$

The formulas is homogeneous. Calculating the expected loss relative to the 0-coupon raises the question of the actualization factor and is equivalent to the pricing of an assurance against this loss.

If the assurance is perfect, that is if it compensates exactly in term of cash flow and event of default, if it is liquid and if one accepts that it replicates the risk free bond, its price would allow to deduct by arbitrage the market value of the expected loss.

It is exactly equal to the difference between the risk free bond and the risky bond:

$$EL_{arbitrated\ market}(t) = e^{-r.t} - (1-LGD).\frac{h}{r+\mu+h}.\left[1-e^{-(r+\mu+h).t}\right] - e^{-(r+\mu+h).t}$$

The fact that markets aren't pure and perfect doesn't prevent to use arbitrage pricing methodologies.

Actually, markets aren't perfect as we have seen and such an insurance doesn't exist. Instead, market can offer financial guarantees and CDS.

Ex ante provisioning

In realty also, h(t) isn't constant over time since at inception, the debtor is supposed to be capable to pay its debts. In another way, the debtor has an initial capital used to build subordination for the debt. Usually, defaults come after a certain period of time and then reduce since they are related to a project and if this one is successful, the debtor generates profits which enhance the subordination of the banker. Regulator requires banks to reserve ex-ante the return corresponding to h.dt in order to smooth this effect over time at each period of time dt.

Indeed before default, for a zero-coupon expiring at time T, the incomes statement and balance sheet has the following evolution for LGD at 100%, at time t < T:

	Value at t	evolution
Price of the bond	$P(t) = E\left[S_t.e^{-(r+\mu)(T-t)}\right] = e^{-(r+\mu+h)(T-t)}$	$dP(t) = (r+\mu+h).e^{-(r+\mu+h)(T-t)}.dt$
Revenues	$P(t) - P(0) = e^{-(r+\mu+h)(T-t)} - e^{-(r+\mu+h).T}$	$dP(t) = (r+\mu+h).e^{-(r+\mu+h)(T-t)}.dt$
Reserves	$R(t) = -\dfrac{h}{r+\mu+h}.\left[P(t) - P(0)\right]$	$dR(t) = -h.e^{-(r+\mu+h)(T-t)}.dt$
Incomes	$I(t) = \dfrac{r+\mu}{r+\mu+h}.\left[P(t) - P(0)\right]$	$dI(t) = (r+\mu).e^{-(r+\mu+h)(T-t)}.dt$

In case of default at time t, the loss is logically $-P(t) - R(t) + I(t) = P(0)$

If the bond is repaid at time T, the bank get an exceptional additional revenue from the reversal of provision.

Pricing of CDS and insurance guarantees

A financial guarantee is an insurance contract under which the insurer, supposed to be a very solid risk, gives the insurance to substitute itself to the debtor in case of default of this one.

By buying the insurance, the bond holder get a bond with a better risk since both the debtor and the insurer must default for him to lose money.

If the insurer were risk free, the sum of the value of the insurance V_t and the bond would be a risk free bond, therefore a natural pricing would be: $P_t + V_t = e^{-r.t}$ out of the margin of the insurer.

This arbitrage approach has limits. The seller of the insurance can hedge itself by borrowing the bonds for a fees and sell it short. But for that, it needs to be able to find the bond, pay the borrowing fee and reinvest the cash in risk free assets. So the price it shall charge for the insurance shall be higher than this theoretical price and actually most of the time $P_t + V_t \leq e^{-r.t}$ (it can be the reverse in specific market conditions).

The actualized expectation of loss of a bond insurance (« expected pay-off ») is the same since one pays LGD in case of default. Only the cash, the financial guarantees and the CDS markets aren't one single markets, the actors are different, their capacities are different, so the risk premium is different.

Concerning the expected pay-off, the actualization factor may include a spread which represents the spread at which the insurer would borrow the money to pay the sinister from its point of view. For the insured, the spread corresponds to the credit risk it faces with the insurer:

$$E\left[PayOff_{insurance}(t)\right] = LGD.\int_0^t h.e^{-(r+\beta+h).s} ds = LGD.\frac{h}{r+\beta+h}.\left[1-e^{-(r+\beta+h).t}\right]$$

Actually, the premium isn't paid at inception but the insurance is purchased against the payment of a premium until the date of eventual default or, if no default occurs, until expiration of the contract. Let write c the instantaneous rate of premium. The insured pays $c.ds$ at each time s before default of the issuer. The expected premium equals with the risk premium β' on the investment of the premium (β' can be negative) by the insurer selling the guarantee and the credit risk of the insured. Actually, since the guarantee disappears in case of non-payment of the premium, this second effect can be neglicted:

$$premium = \int_0^t \left(\int_0^s c.e^{-(r+\beta').u} .du \right) .h.e^{-h.s} .ds + c.S_t. \int_0^t e^{-(r+\beta').u} .du$$

$$premium = c. \frac{1-e^{-(r+\beta'+h).t}}{r+\beta'+h}$$

The actualization factors are different between the actualized value of the sinister and the premium. Usually, it is neglected but we added it because in some market conditions, it can be significant. This is especially true if the risk on the insurer is significant. The market practice is actually to neglect this risk in the pricing of the contract and price it separately through CVA. Note that CVA also include a risk premium which makes the whole structure even more complex!

At date 0, loss and premium must balance out of insurer profit margin, which allows us to deduct the spread of the CDS:

$$LGD. \frac{h}{r+\beta+h} . \left[1 - e^{-(r+\beta+h).t} \right] = c. \frac{1-e^{-(r+\beta'+h).t}}{r+\beta'+h}$$

If both risk premium are identical, one gets $c = h.LGD$. This is the case in our example of pure and perfect markets.

If not, one get:
$$c = h.LGD. \frac{r+\beta'+h}{r+\beta+h} . \frac{1-e^{-(r+\beta+h).t}}{1-e^{-(r+\beta'+h).t}}$$

For t small, the two formulas are equivalent. With a bid/ask spread of 0.5%, the difference in the estimation of h remains small in our testing and we will negligee the difference of spread.

What we observe is that the market isn't balanced most of the time. Usually, the availability of insurance is reduced, the availability of arbitrage is also limited. Therefore, we add a margin m to the CDS coupon. This margin can be positive or negative depending on the market. Most of the time, it is positive.

$$c = h.LGD + m$$

It is interesting to observe that so far, the insurance contract doesn't integrate the risk premium on the bond.

The default of this formula is that LGD is also a random variable. Please notice that during the 2008 crisis, models with deterministic LGD became irrelevant in the situation of observed stress and teams tried to develop models with random recovery, in order to better explain prices.

The value of the CDS is equal to the difference between expected loss and premium:

$$V(c) = \frac{1-e^{-(r+h)t}}{r+h}.(h.LGD - c)$$

At inception, it should be negative equal to:

$$V_{0,t} = -\frac{1-e^{-(r+h)t}}{r+h}.m_{0,t}$$

This express the fact that the insured is paying a premium to the insurer in addition of the best estimate of the sinister.

Actually, the market doesn't price CDS and financial guarantees by seeking to estimate h and the risk margin and therefore overvalue the price of the protection at inception. This methodology allows the seller of the insurance to hide its margin. It is a classical methodology used by investment banks to hide the margin they make on any structured products. The value they provide to their customers is always overestimated for two reasons: they don't want to take the profit up-front and they don't want the customer to see the profit.

A better and more transparent solution would be for them to value properly the contract, reserve the profit margin at inception as insurers do and revert it progressively over the time life of the product.

The variation of value of the CDS at time t can come from a change in value of h, LGD or m.

$$\Delta MtM = V(c) - V(c_m) = c \cdot \frac{1-e^{-(r+h)t}}{r+h} - c_m \cdot \frac{1-e^{-(r+h_m)t}}{r+h_m}$$

If one assumes h constant (the intrinsic risk doesn't change), the variation of value of the CDS is independent from the LGD but includes the variation of margin m.

$$\Delta MtM = V(c) - V(c_m) = (c - c_m) \cdot \frac{1-e^{-(r+h)t}}{r+h} = (m - m_m) \cdot \frac{1-e^{-(r+h)t}}{r+h}$$

At inception, the pay-off of the 0-coupon plus the CDS must be closed to the risk free 0-coupon, if the market has sufficient liquidity in first approximation:

$$e^{-r.t} = (1-LGD) \cdot \frac{h}{r+\mu+h} \cdot \left[1 - e^{-(r+\mu+h)t}\right] + e^{-(r+\mu+h)t} + m \cdot \frac{1-e^{-(r+h)t}}{r+h}$$

Where $m \cdot \frac{1-e^{-(r+h)t}}{r+h}$ is the initial margin V_0.

In our model, the spread of the cash bond is $spread_{cash} = h + \mu$ and the spread of the insurance is $spread_{cds} = h.LGD + m$. So we get the relationship between both spreads (first approximation):

$$e^{-r.t} = (1-LGD) \cdot \frac{h}{r+spread_{cash}} \cdot \left[1 - e^{-(r+spread_{cash})t}\right] + e^{-(r+spread_{cash})t} + (spread_{cds} - h.LGD) \frac{1-e^{-(r+h)t}}{r+h}$$

20

Where $V_0 = \left(spread_{cds} - h.LGD\right)\dfrac{1-e^{-(r+h).t}}{r+h}$

For *LGD* = 100% and *t* small, one get $m = \mu$ in first approximation.

In all the other case, the spread of cash and CDS are simply different as was observed during the crisis. Their difference, called the "base", can move significantly and in an asymmetrical way:

- if an insurer of good quality wrongly price the CDS below the cash spread, an investor will have the interest of buying the bond and paying the CDS, locking a margin. That's what is called a negative basis trade when $spread_{cds} \leq spread_{cash}$. The position is not risk free from a MTM point of view since the base can move. However, during a crisis, the base usually get back positive since the CDS reacts faster than the cash. This is at the advantage of the NBT owner. However, interest rates are usually getting down and CVA on the insurer increases which reduces its profit MtM.
- The reverse position is very difficult to build (selling the CDS and hedging by borrowing and selling the bond short) and the base can move significantly on the positive side.

Nota: there are, as for interest rates, more sophisticated models for the rate of default *h(t)*. The most used is the following:

$h(t) = E\left[h(t)\right].h_t^{bk}$ where h_t^{bk} is Black-Karasinski Brownian process: $d\ln h_t^{bk} = -k.\ln h_t^{bk}.dt + \sigma.dB_t$

The models try to link then the risk premium with the volatility of *h*.

This doesn't change the fundamental idea of this paper which is that there is a risk premium charged in addition of *h* which can move significantly and jump in period of crisis.

Estimating the probability of default $h(t)$ and margin $\mu(t)$

There is an abundant literature about the subject. It distinguishes two types of model:

- Models of default probability derived from stock equity observations following Vasicek-Kealhofer paper. These models see the price of the stock as an option on the market asset value of the company, with a strike equals to liabilities. The company defaults when the value of assets follow below this strike. Model provides a probability of defaulting and an indication of volatility of the assets deducted from the equity volatility which can be used for the risk premium.
- Reduced-form models which deduct the probability of default from the credit spread trying to explain the risk premium in a kind of CAPM approach linking volatility and risk premium.

Both models are useful. However, both miss to catch the very specific way the credit market is working. Prices are made by men who use the same economic approach but with high flexibility:

- They compare spreads between classes and ratings and inside classes per name,
- They take into account their capital and liquidity needs and their expectation of profitability,
- They try to maximize their profit especially when they know there isn't real competition,
- They can panic and get out of the market under pressure like in the crisis.

The market provide information on the spreads but prices don't give most of time direct information to LGD, μ and h. Note that sometimes they do: for names with clean subordination of debt trading on CDS, one get additional equations to estimate LGD. Furthermore, other financial elements can help get rough estimates.

Let get back to our example and try to understand what happened during the crisis in the surprisingly high moves observed on its CDS. The truce is that during the crisis, the last market making desks still operating where in banks and so applying a classical banking pricing approach. Indeed, the profitability of the lending business is pretty easy to follow by analyzing banks' annual reports. Applying these metrics to the corporate lending business shows a remarkably stable situation for our example. We have here deducted to hazard rate before crisis from the returns banks were generating on the business and looked if by adapting to the post crisis parameters (that is same expenses, more capital, higher refunding, higher spread, stable return), the difference was coming from a variation of the hazard rate or of the risk premium. In our case, most of the variation relates to the risk premium.

		before crisis	after crisis
(1)	spread over LIBOR	0.20%	0.80%
(2)	spread of refunding	0.00%	0.50%
(3)	financial incomes (2) - (1)	0.20%	0.30%
(4)	commissions linked to lending activity	0.03%	0.03%
(5)	revenues of lending (3) + (4)	**0.23%**	**0.33%**
(6)	expenses	-0.09%	-0.09%
(7)	incomes before risk (5) - (6)	0.14%	0.24%
(8)	cost of risk	-0.02%	-0.02%
(9)	**LGD**	30.00%	30.00%
(10)	**hazard rate h**	0.07%	0.07%
(11)	net incomes (7) - (8)	0.12%	0.22%
(12)	RWA	100.00%	100.00%
(13)	core tiers one solvency ratio	4.00%	8.00%
(14)	allocated core equity tiers one (10) * (11)	4.00%	8.00%
(15)	**excess return over RFR on capital (9) / (12)**	2.93%	2.72%
(16)	**implied risk premium m (1) - (2) - (10)**	0.13%	0.23%

Estimates of commissions, expenses and cost of risk are ratios extrapolated from annual reports of banks on their corporate lending activities.

Estimations are rough but remind also that **in the composition of spreads** before as well as after the crisis, **most of it is still the excess margin**. The increase of the risk margin has all the explanations already mentioned and on the graph, clearly the spread is much more volatile justifying a higher premium too. Between the two phenomena, it isn't possible to differentiate. Also the banks' behavior is linked to their own spread, which is linked to the higher volatility of the names they have in portfolio: banks are indeed providing us additional informations on the fundamental economic risks.

Another interesting observation is that **the estimation of h is much lower than what is provided by rating agencies for BBB+ bonds** translating the fact that the rating itself isn't necessary the best predictor of the probability of default but the class and stability in the class is much more relevant.

Finally, by reverse-engineering the excess return over RFR after the crisis on our example, it is clear that the risk of the bonds didn't deteriorate: its economic attractiveness is similar and asking an institution with a solid funding to take a MtM loss on this bond would make non-sense.

Another example of the influence of the market on the spread of credit is the quasi-automatic widening observed when a paper is downgraded from investment grade to Non-investment grade. The traditional explanation is that, even though all information was on the market before the decision of the rating agencies, there were still a degree of uncertainty justifying a better spread, before the decision was implemented. In reality, this explanation may not be the only one and the mechanisms of limits and/or additional capital requirements on NIG for most of the institutional investors generate automatic decisions of sale. Traditional investors in the NIG environment are different, price differently their risks and have less capacity. In addition, they know the market is in their direction. The movements observed during a downgrade to NIG are indeed related for a large part to the segregation between the two markets.

The risk premium in the credit world is defined by the market. However, market participants do have the classical approach of ranking the names to define which appear more volatile than the others. Therefore, there is a level of homogeneity in the risk premium as what is described by the CAPM models: credit with higher volatility of their probability of default, which translate in a higher volatility of their CDS require a higher risk premium.

Conclusion

The modeling of the realty is extremely simple and natural. It explains most of the erratic movements observed in the MtM of bonds, including utilities. In period of crisis, insurers are moved out of the market, the remaining insurers or the new entering (usually hedge funds) adjust their prices aggressively in order to take a sufficient margin of safety in front of the adverse environment. Prices collapse much more than the variation of expected loss could explain.

This phenomena isn't in contradiction with economic theory. Just the arbitrages mechanisms are sometimes no longer working. The notion of risk premium is natural for equity, natural for loans (that's how banks make their money) but too often forgotten in the pricing of bonds. The analogy between CDS pricing and equity pricing generates also confusion sometimes: the risk-neutral probability of the B&S models defines a link between the derivatives and the cash market under the assumption of absence of arbitrage opportunity. It doesn't remove the risk premium on equity in the "real" probability world. The phenomena is identical with CDS but in addition, arbitrages are much less feasible and the derivative market is much more compartmented from the cash, especially in period of crisis. By adding one additional element in the composition of the credit spreads, our methodology doesn't put anymore in competition the "reduced-form models" using credit spreads to determine the probability of default from the Vasicek-Kealhofer using the equity information. It is even likely that both models can be integrated into a global one. However, we still believe that the mechanism of banking leverage shall be taken into account to complete the system of equations. If not, both models face difficulties distinguishing independent market parameters from structural changes in the risk of a debtor.

Indeed, the calculation of the best estimate faces the difficulty that anticipated $h(t)$ and LGD aren't available directly from markets' data and financial statements. Their segregation from the risk premium is not possible using only instantaneous market information. However, this raises a very serious challenge against the new tendency for full MtM, since sometimes, the market doesn't translate the real economic variation of the intrinsic value but only the changes in trading conditions between actors.

SELLING A NON PERFORMING UNSECURED RETAIL LOANS BOOK: strategic considerations and methodology of pricing

The sale of non-performing loans isn't a standard operation for financial institutions: it has to be thoroughly considered and integrated into a global strategy. This memorandum describes the independent methodology ALM-Vision uses to price NPL retail trades (as defined article 7. "claims included in the regulatory retail portfolio" of the Basel II regulation[1] so out of mortgages) and discuss the different parameters in order to optimize the trade for both parties, buyer and seller.

We review first the parameters involved in the pricing, we then give an example and in the second part, we discuss the conditions for matching the interests of buyers and sellers to get a trade that makes sense for both. We choose to introduce the matter on pricing first despite the fact that pricing is the most technical aspect because it is a key element to understand the nature of these trades. The reader interested in the strategic motivations of a trade can however just review these elements and focus on the last part of the memorandum.

Valuation of Non Performing Loans

Parameters involved

Non Performing Loans ("NPL") are considered as receivables. Their pricing is a classical cash flow pricing exercise integrating refunding costs (as for ABS). Indeed, the different parameters included in the pricing are:

- The average expected time set of cash flow: this is obviously the key element and the one having the highest influence on the pricing of the deal. It is also the one translating the added

---

[1] BCBS128 page 23

value of the buyer, its expertise, and the quality of its systems. Obviously, it is also the most difficult to model since each loan has to be renegotiated and this results in a new amortizing schedule. The more information the buyer gets and the more experienced it is, the better the modeling.

- ✓ The first parameter is the type of loans, their general characteristics: market, customer profiles, criteria of underwriting, existence of an address, deceased...
- ✓ The second parameter is the status of the loan: paying or not paying.
- ✓ The third parameter is the age in default: primary for less than 91 days, secondary until 2 years, tertiary after...
- ✓ The fourth parameter is the work which has already been done on the file.

Experience shows that the older the claim, the higher the expertise and work required. Indeed, even the biggest consumer loan houses in Europe consider recovery of these type of claims as a different business than their core one and are always more regularly selling their old files, rather than building a full infrastructure to maximize their recovery. In addition, there is often a psychological effect for the borrower when he or she gets informed that his or her file is no longer handled by its lender but has been transferred to a specialized entity. Indeed, the recovery expectation of specialized entities is usually higher than the one from the bank. At least, there are high economies of scale in the recovery business.

Modeling the expected cash flow is done through statistical analysis based on past observations. When past experiences aren't available, houses use similar data to what they have in their historical records (several millions of files for the biggest specialized houses). The underwriting criteria are indeed key to try to find similar customer profiles to get an estimate of their behavior (but these criteria may change from time to time). The best information one can get is the history of each file: that is the regularity of the payments already done (every month, every quarter) and age of the loan (paying since 12 months, just 3 months..., having stopped paying three months ago...). The more regular the payments, the higher the probability that the regularity of payments lasts. Using this information, models give an estimation of expected future cash flows[2]. In general, the more experienced buyers are, the better they price in a market where sometimes new entrants can disrupt pricing.

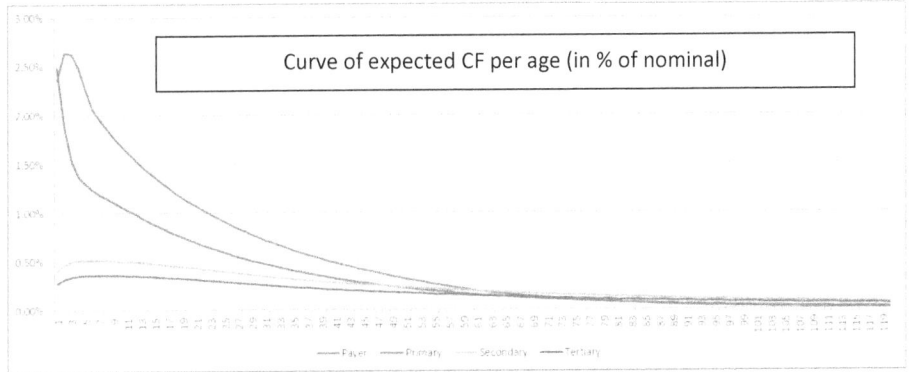

- Cost of recovery. These costs can be pretty significant, especially for old files for which contact information is no longer available. Their modeling depends on the buyer. The simplest modeling express them as a percentage of collection. This is often insufficient and reality is a mix of fixed costs, employee time costs and external costs (Baillie, legal...). Fixed and indirect costs are high at the beginning of the deal since the new team needs to feed the system of the buyer with information and initiate contact with the borrowers. There again, experience is key and economies of scale can be massive, including cost of Baillie. Experience is also key in order to maximize the revenue net from the files: the buyer will have indeed to define its strategy between legal

---

[2] Usually, pricing doesn't try to model the different states of each file, since payers can stop paying and resume payments.

procedures, speed agreement... The classical strategy uses a simple matrix:

Borrower...	Wants to pay	Doesn't want to
can pay	Agree on a reasonable clean	Legal fight
can't pay	Patience[3]. Reducing debt.	Wait and

Specialized houses have developed extremely sophisticated processes and systems to optimize the work of their teams, reducing these costs as much as possible. They use sophisticated algorithms to classify their debtors and define the optimum strategy of collection. These methodologies aren't available to most of the banks and explain the difference in collection costs.

- Interest rate curve for actualization of cash flows. We use E3M or OIS market data depending on refunding rules.

- Spread of refunding. That is the spread at which the buyer is able to refund part of its purchase. Obviously banking entities and insurance companies have an advantage.

- Leverage used by the buyer. That is the amount of capital the buyer put in the deal. By experience, the highest leverage is generated by banking entities. Under Basel II rules (paragraph 10[4]), unreserved part of past due loans (91 days and above) is by default weighted at 150% with some exemptions:
    - If more than 20% of the loan is already reserved, 100% weighting.
    - If more than 50% of the loan is already reserved, 50% weighting may be allowed at the discretion of the regulator.

---

[3] Most difficulties come from « life accidents »: death, divorce, loss of job, accidents, diseases... Statistically, one observes that most borrowers with this profile recover after 5 to 7 years and are eager to reimburse their debts, after a reasonable agreement.
[4] BCBS 128 page 25

Some regulators like the Swedish regulators provide also the possibility to treat purchased NPL as simple receivables, granting them a general 100% RWA (paragraph 12 other assets).

- Actualization spread of the cash flow: this is a pure market parameter as with any ABS expressing the uncertainty in the cash flow. Hedge funds opportunistic buyers of NPL focus on this parameter compared to other investments they may choose. The parameter depends indeed on the asset class, the history of the seller and the market. It mostly translates the level of uncertainty in the estimation of cash flows (uncertain CF, CF far in the future are applied a higher spread). NPL portfolios are obviously non rated structures. However, for professionals of the domain, volatility of cash flow is better known and less correlated with the global economic situation than for equity tranches of CDO. Therefore, actualization spreads are currently relatively low, which explains also the number of operations observed. Another interesting effect explains the relatively low spreads: these trades are very similar to CDO equity in the way that the law of probability for the repartition of the actualized cash flow is relatively symmetrical, which isn't the case for other ABS tranches (asymmetry compensated by the spread received). It is difficult to give rules since each portfolio is different and prices depend on the leverage available. However, as a matter of fact:
    - ✓ Most regular and reliable pricing are provided by specialist houses (in Europe, mainly HOIST and EOS) which don't have refunding issues (since they are banks), which use stable leverage and do not have opportunistic behavior.
    - ✓ Hedge funds and investment banks' opportunist buyers seem to compare the return to a portfolio of non-investment grade bonds, around BB.

These deals are more complex and sensitive than classical portfolio sales and price is not the only element to consider.

Pricing

The calculation is straight forward given these parameters and result in a selling price as in the following example:

year	0	1	2	3	4	5	6	7
nominal (M€)	100.00	60.00	39.42	29.59	24.81	22.52	21.49	21.00
Cash flows collected (M€)		16.00	7.20	2.95	1.19	0.46	0.15	0.05
var. collection costs per file (€)	50	50	50	60	70	60	50	50
fixed costs (M€)		-1	-0.9	-0.8	-0.6	-0.2	0	0
var. costs per file (M€)		-1.40	-0.74	-0.41	-0.29	-0.20	-0.10	-0.05
collection costs (M€)		-2.40	-1.64	-1.21	-0.89	-0.40	-0.10	-0.05
Net collection (M€)		13.6	5.6	1.7	0.3	0.1	0.1	0.0
IR		0.076%	0.094%	0.143%	0.221%	0.325%	0.455%	0.591%
Zero-coupon Euribor		99.92%	99.81%	99.57%	99.12%	98.39%	97.31%	95.96%
Zero-coupon with receivable spread		95.17%	90.54%	86.03%	81.58%	77.15%	72.71%	68.33%
BV of receivables (M€)	19.81	4.82	0.00	0.00	0.00	0.00	0.00	0.00
Capital required	2.97	0.72	0.00	0.00	0.00	0.00	0.00	0.00
funding required	16.84	3.34	0.00	0.00	0.00	0.00	0.00	0.00
spread of funding		0.5%	0.5%	0.5%	0.5%	0.5%	0.5%	0.5%
spread of receivable		5.0%	5.0%	5.0%	5.0%	5.0%	5.0%	5.0%
cost of funding		-0.10	-0.02	0.00	0.00	0.00	0.00	0.00
earnings before amortization		13.50	5.55	1.74	0.31	0.06	0.05	0.00
notional interest on receivable		1.01	0.25	0.00	0.00	0.00	0.00	0.00
amortizing		-14.99	-4.82	0.00	0.00	0.00	0.00	0.00
incomes		-1.49	0.73	1.74	0.31	0.06	0.05	0.00
asset cash flow	-19.81	13.50	5.55	1.74	0.31	0.06	0.05	0.00
treasury	-2.97	0.00	2.21	1.74	0.31	0.06	0.05	0.00
ROE	16%							

A ROE of 16% on such a deal is actually very reasonable since it is before taking into account any overhead structure of the buyer. It is relatively similar to standard banking activities. Buyers without leverage will just focus on the actualization spread of the receivables. In our example, the spread is around 5%. This spread is defined by the market in comparison to similar risks.

Strategic motivations of a sale

The motivation behind the decision of selling NPL is a mix of several elements:

- The price compared to the choice of managing the files internally, including the cost of immobilized capital,
- The absolute level of NPL in the book and records: especially in a period of recession, banks may have an interest not to show increasing amount of CDL by cleaning their balance sheet,
- The willingness and capacity to invest in an activity which is no longer related to the commercial franchise and which requires always more expensive investments in training, processes and systems,
- The strategic willingness to share or exit the risk related to an activity which is no longer linked to the franchise (that is real customers) and to build long term ties with a partner willing to step in at times of difficulty.

Optimum date of sale

Banks don't use the same reserving models than the net expected cash flow curve used by specialized buyers. Usually, they just reserve the expected loss after only direct costs (that is the costs paid to Baillie and lawyers) without necessary actualizing and usually without taking into account the actualization spread (which translate the uncertainty of recovery).

As a result, banks selling new NPL most of time have to take a loss out of specific structuration aspects of the deal (to avoid this kind of situation the most sophisticated houses have a different reserving policy closer to market prices).

If after 6 to 12 months, the bank has not been able to resolve the situation, it usually takes a more cautious provisioning and increases this one until the recovery team gives up any hope of recovery. Indeed, there is an optimum time for selling: this is the time at which the reserve made by the bank equals the discount requested by buyers to buy the file. This optimum usually exist since the expected loss curve of banks fall relatively quickly to zero after 12 months whereas buyers with expertise in recovery of old files still price them accordingly.

The table below shows an example of the different approaches to pricing. In this case, the bank has an obvious interest to sell the NPL after 6 months:

TYPE	AGE	TOTAL COLLECTIONS	COSTS ASSUMED	NET PRICE	BANK ESTIMATED LOSS	BANK ESTIMATED DIRECT COST	BANK RESERVES	BANK IMPLIED PRICE
PAYER		61%	20%	46%	30%	10%	37%	63
PRIMARY	<6 months	41%	20%	31%	65%	10%	68.5%	31.5
SECONDARY	<24 months	28%	20%	22%	80%	10%	82%	18
TERTIARY	>24 months	21%	20%	16%	100%	0%	100%	0

Processes for efficient recovery become always more sophisticated and complex to implement and the trend is not going to reverse with the additional pressure made by the regulator and the politicians on a subject culturally seen as negative in most societies. Indeed, specialized houses now show recoveries which can be up to 30% more efficient than in house performances.

However, economically, banks sometimes do not take into account indirect costs and costs of staffing because they consider that they are independent of the sale or not of the files. This isn't a correct approach and the strategy of selling or not, if it isn't opportunistic, allows entities to avoid investments in systems and teams since they systematically sell the files.

Indeed, the optimum for transferring a file appears to be more the date at which the bank considers the customer as lost. In this case, it makes sense for it to just **transfer the recovery to a specialized entity since the activity is no longer related to its customers' franchise**. It is then the responsibility of the bank to adapt its workforce to the new strategy. The seller can participate in this adjustment by taking over some of the teams.

Advantages and risks of a sale

Banks usually reserve without taking directly into account the uncertainty in the recovery expressed in the actualization spread. However, they usually take a margin of safety (if not, this isn't a good sign). The spread reflects the market price for the risk of not being able to recover the expected amount, in the same way as the banks take a margin of safety. **When a bank decides not to sell and handle the recovery, it is actually making a strong strategic decision to assume this uncertainty and mobilize the required capital.**

Regular sale also usually allows for the improvement of the cost/income ratio of an institution since banks no longer have to manage the files. Keep in mind that costs of managing NPL are extremely high, between 18% in a specialized institution up to 30% for small banks. This fact explains also the current trend for institutions to implement regular strategic sales: there is a clear industrialisation of the business with a concentration in term of actors and a specializing. **Banks outsourcing this activity make the strategic decision to focus on its customer franchise.**

Indeed, banks know perfectly that a customer is lost after six months of unsuccessful attempt to settle the situation. The NPL files aren't a commercial issue anymore and can be sold without damaging the commercial franchise. However, **there is a reputational risk in the sale and the buyer must comply with the ethical standards** expected by the seller in order to avoid any reputational damage: the name of the seller remains in the files and for the public, sales are still considered first as a decision of the bank to externalize recovery. In a market where many collection agencies are small entities without necessarily regulation and too often an incentive to implement aggressive collections strategies, this can become a major issue. Subsequently, many institutions now **request from the buyer state of the art and ethically irreproachable procedures and the commitment not to resell the loans.**

Another issue banks have before selling loans is the loss of expertise and information about an activity which is still intrinsic to their business: banks want to keep the information about the recovery, first because it allows to double-check the price at which selling and second because it gives a complete economic view on their credit activity. Actually, there are three genuine answers to these points:

- since the banks still handle the recovery for the first months, usually six months, they need to keep some teams and expertise and **actually maintain the most crucial part of recovery: the first six months indeed proved to be key for a successful recovery** because it is during this period that the lender has the ability to identify the origin of the default and its solution and to actively try to solve quickly the issue.
- If they want to maintain the expertise in term of collection of older files, they still have the possibility to keep a certain percentage of the files to be managed internally.
- Finally, the contract of sale can include a covenant under which the buyer commits to provide the seller with regular reports on its collection per file. This simple rule allows banks to appreciate ex-post the performance of a pool they sold.

Regular sales are virtuous in many additional ways if they are implemented wisely.

- First, it forces the institutions to focus on the recovery when it is still possible to save the customer.
- It also forces the institution to reserve properly from the beginning, which is a constant request from the regulators.
- It maintains a very clean balance sheet.
- If the bank chooses long term reliable partners, the strategy of regular sale is a safety net for the period of problems: during these times, opportunistic buyers disappear or have a tendency to increase strongly their prices and reduce their capacities, whereas specialized buyers remain constant. This point is indeed extremely important by experience and sometimes the best price isn't the best deal. Banks must be beware of the opportunistic sales strategies.

Different types of sales

Sales can take different forms depending on the situation of the customer:

- ✓ Classical sale consists in selling for a fixed price the book to a specialized entity. This solution is clean and simple, even though as we have seen some covenants are always delicate to negotiate: reporting, interdiction of resale, definition of the eligible files, definition of the work made on files before transfer... In this kind of transaction, the key element is the impact of the sale on the incomes of the bank. That is the difference between the market price of the NPL and their valuation in the books of the bank.

- ✓ "Buy and leave" sales are a true sale to an investor but the management of the files is still handled by the bank. This solution is attractive when the bank can't get rid of the team or wants to keep the expertise internally. It is also adapted in small markets where the investors have no strategic interest in having a local collection agency or for markets where selling NPL isn't in use and no collection agency of quality exists. Buy and Leave are first a way of cleaning the balance sheet. The price can be adjusted around de facto 20 to 25% by deciding or not to integrate the cost of recovery in the pricing: the buyer can indeed agree to buy, let's say 20% more but in exchange shall not be re-invoiced for the internal costs of the bank. Buy and leave deals make more sense if the buyer has a sufficient expertise to help improve the collection process. Some deals include an option for the buyer to later buy the team and systems in order for it to set up its own operations.

- ✓ Sale with transfer of team: the buyer makes the acquisition of the portfolio and in parallel accepts to hire the team managing it and eventually acquire its systems. This solution allows the bank to truly get rid of all the costs related to the transferred activity. The process needs to follow the legal procedure for the transfer of team and the pricing shall integrate these elements.

- ✓ Sale with an option to return to profit, or a profit sharing clause... This kind of clause is aimed at aligning the interests of both parties. They are mostly used in markets where prices are uncertain and actualization spread is high.

- ✓ Forward sale: forward sale of future flow of NPL at a pre-agreed price is the natural consequence of the strategic decision by the bank to get rid of the activity. Forward sale has the advantage for the bank to eliminate the uncertainty since the price is fixed, conditionally to the fact that the files match pre-agreed criteria. In a global deal on the stock and forward, it gives one additional parameter to avoid a potential up front loss.

All these possibilities can obviously be combined to get the most adapted solution to the specific needs of a bank.

MODELING and PRICING PREPAYMENTS: *a market approach*

(Serge Moulin, Olivier Moreau)

Introduction

Prepayments have been the subject of abundant literature with the development of RMBS but remain one of the most complex subject in finance. The risk is well known. They are loan renegotiations and anticipated prepayments decided by the clients following a lowering in the interest rates and effected without penalty (or with a lower penalty than that of the market value variation). In the case of a lowering of interest rates, the prepayments naturally induce a loss of future earnings for the bank or even bring about a direct loss, particularly in case of market refinancing.

Of course, banks are aware of the phenomenon that can amplify in size in case of a major movement in interest rates but they are still having difficulties in modelling it and evaluating it even though the phenomenon can have massive consequences in terms of cash flow (see graphic below).

After introducing the effect of prepayments and mechanisms involved in this phenomena, we provide some fundamental elements of prepayment modeling and effects. We then present a solution in order to price the implicit option, using market parameters, for different shapes of behavioral curves.

Our model has the advantage of being calibrated with market parameters. This is a necessity in order to get realistic prices and proper hedging strategy.

Cash flows generated by a loan pool with constant annuity of an initial duration of 12 years.

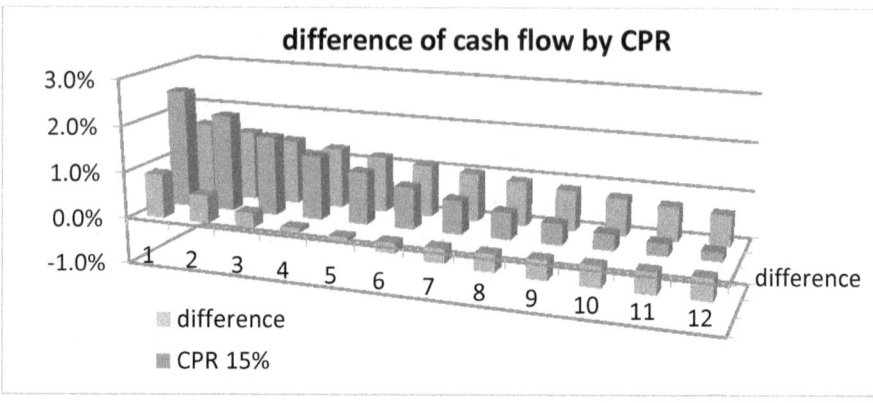

Elements influencing prepayments

The prepayment or renegotiation behavior modeling is a delicate exercise. We can distinguish two types of repurchases:

• Structural prepayments are independent of interest rates or economic cycle: These decisions are often linked to life events: unexpected revenue incomes (inheritances...), divorces, deaths, accidents, births (purchase of a larger house), children leaving home, move from region... These events are mostly independent of the economic cycle and they are easy to take into account as they reduce the true duration of a loan pool. Depending on the markets, this phenomenon can convey between 2% to 8% to the remaining nominal each year. It is therefore a fundamental phenomenon and an error in its estimation will have a greater impact than, for example, an error in the cash flows related to a pool of credit products on a market over a quarter for an initial duration of 8 to 12 years.

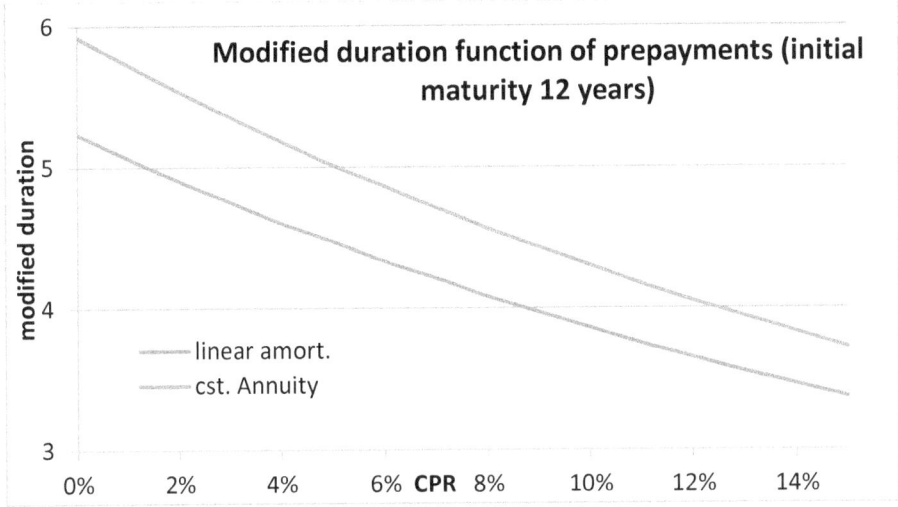

- Prepayments linked to the economic cycle, and particularly to the interest rates: during a period of decrease in the rates, if the client does not pay a penalty at market price, he/she would be best to exercise his/her option and repay in anticipation, ready to contract a new loan. A decrease in rates is often in fact linked to a recession situation and therefore to an increase in non-performing loans, which worsens the situation of the bank. Inversely, during a period of increase in rates, clients that have the opportunity to repay by anticipation (due to an unexpected cash income for example) would be best to keep their loan and invest their funds. The rate of anticipated repayments is therefore lowered.

The factors that influence the prepayment rate of clients are traditionally:

- The market value of the difference in rates with the new market conditions (the rate difference multiplied by the sensitivity): this is the most important factor. However, actually, one observes that customers are more sensitive to the variation in rates (independently of the modified duration) than the MtM as it is difficult for them to estimate.
- Credit size: Clients with a higher income tend to take larger credits and, more often, and more efficiently, perform a rate comparison

and decide on arbitrating the bank. Prepayments can generate fixed costs (on the guarantees for example) or even hidden costs (even if it is just the time taken for the operation) which are lower in proportion to the nominal. Regarding real estate, credits lower than €100,000 that are repaid in anticipation occur half as much as credits of €200,000 or more.
- The threshold effect known as 'Media effect': borrowers have a higher tendency to renegotiate their credits when the rates approach historic lows. The wave intensity of repurchasing is also greater if the lower threshold is older and media discuss it.
- The credit spread and the risk: the riskier the customer, the larger the original spread, the weaker the probability for renegotiation. This is linked to the client characteristics: higher risk, more loyal, less discerning about the price, less sought out by competitors, less comfortable having a new negotiation with his or her bank... In the same manner, government-sponsored loans are more stable.
- The age of the loans, indeed there is usually few prepayments at the beginning and at the end of a loan (the customers let their loan die).
- The burnout effect: there is an exhaustion effect and customers who have already exercised their option have a lower probability to do it again. In a same way, when interest rates decrease, there is a peak of prepayments after which the prepayment rate reduces: like a wave, customers exercise their options. The ones who did not exercise those have a lower probability of doing so in the future.
- The market environment and competition between banks: management of their salesforce, objectives, policy concerning prepayments... Also markets with high use of loans brokers see higher prepayments rates.

On the real estate market (the most important market for retail banks), other specific factors enter into play:
- Real estate prices impact transaction volume and market activity relating to mortgage credit. In fact, a rising market promotes transactions, often leading to a period of growth and increased

anticipated prepayments (independently of interest rates). Note that real estate prices can also, as was the case with the subprimes, have a direct impact on the claims, and this, even more if the credit was provided on the basis of collateral rather than on the financial situation of the borrower.
- The economic context: an economy undergoing growth promotes mobility and the enrichment of its citizens as well as their trust in the future and therefore their credit decisions (but it can promote inflation that encourages a reverse effect).
- Seasonality is important too with a number of major transactions in the spring, before the end of the school year, that therefore shows a statistical rate of prepayment 2 to 3 points higher than average.

Movements can be massive as shown in the graph below. However, they occur in waves, with customers making the arbitrage relatively quickly if it reaches the level they see as interesting for them to exercise their option.

Historical Prepayment Data (including and excluding Repurchases)

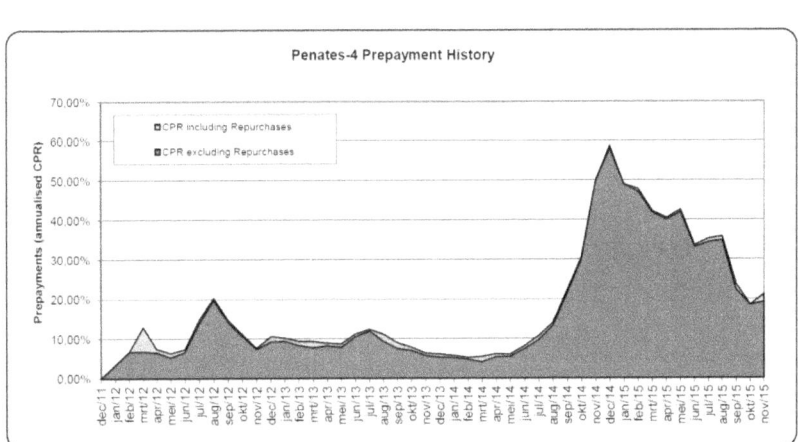

Source: Penates-4 quarterly Investor Report 25-11-2015, courtesy of Belfius.

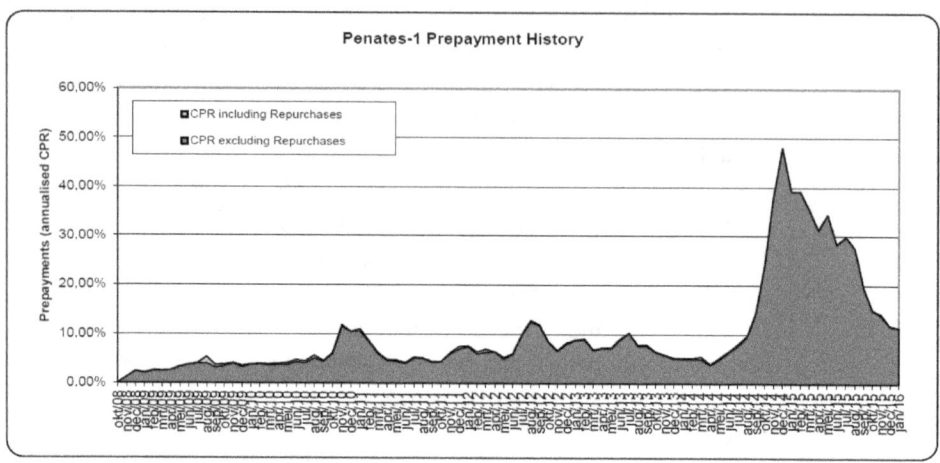

Information from some of our customers shows that prepayment reaction is not that significantly affected by the age of loans (even though there is a sensitivity).

Modeling customer behavior

Formally, customers are the owners of an American option to cancel a swap (if one neglects the spread effect). In theory, if they were rational, they would exercise the day where the intrinsic value is superior to the value of keeping the option. This period can be easily modeled in a simple Cox-Ross tree model. But in reality, customers are not rational professional traders with real time quotes available. Indeed, in the tree, their decision of exercising the option is based on different criteria.

There are two modelling methods for prepayments:

- The loan by loan method.

- The method by credit pooling when the portfolio is sufficiently large that it is possible to reason in terms of percentage.

Markov chain loan by loan modeling

The credit by credit method is used for the securities of 'corporate' credit portfolios or project financing, generally of a larger size and in numbers that are too small for the application of the second method. This method has also been used for the RMBS when the pools were diverse and the models that gave the anticipated repayment probabilities needed to be calculated loan by loan. We typically note $h(t)$ for the instant probability that the remaining capital $CRD(t)$ will be repaid between t and $t+dt$, knowing that this was not the case beforehand. Let note $m(t)$ the standard instalment amount that is without prepayment. $S(t)$ is the survival function, that is the probability that a credit will not lead to an prepayment before t. We therefore have:

$$S(t) = e^{-\int_0^t h(u).du}$$

In t, apart from the risk of default and penalty, the bank receives:

$$\begin{cases} 0 \text{ if } t \geq T \text{ excluding default} \\ m(t) \text{ if reimbursements are normal with the probability } S(t).(1-h(t).dt) \\ m(t)+CRD(t) \text{ if prepayment with the probability } S(t).h(t).dt \end{cases}$$

This method is less well adapted to a retail bank and regards more corporate and investment banks. It is complex to calibrate and usually uses scoring methodologies to determine the probability of prepayment at each date, depending on the characteristic of the loan. The truncation effect (we observe only the loans which are still alive and the past loans) must be taken into account for the estimation of the maximum likelihood (there is abundant literature on this topic).

Pool modeling

The method by credit pooling simply takes into account that a percentage $h(t)$ of $CRD(t)$ is repaid by anticipation on date t. It is adapted to major sized unified loan classes (of over 1,000 loans). This is the method used in the models and output pricing of Freddy Mac and Fanny Mae.

The objective is to define the function h_t that gives the instantaneous percentage of prepayments at time t, that is to say the proportion of clients prepaying their loan according to all the information available on the rate curve since the beginning. It is clear that h_t will have a random combination linked to factors other than the rates that will be difficult to disassociate.

Some useful definitions

The best known market is the American mortgage market with four or five investment banks that, prior to the crisis, maintained highly precise historical databases on their client behavior. With the crisis and the disappearance of two of these banks (Lehman and Bear), the data is less accessible (and less used, which is a pity as the reality remains the same).

The American real estate loan market is also that which enabled the formalisation of the key definitions: SMM, CPR and PSA.

- SMM or 'Single Monthly Mortality' rate measures the prepayments percentage in the month relative to the theoretical nominal at the end of the month (that is to say before prepayments):

$$SMM = 1 - \frac{\text{end of month observed nominal}}{\text{end of month theoretical nominal}} = \frac{\text{prepayments of the month}}{\text{end of month theoretical nominal}}$$

- CPR, or Constant Prepayment Rate, measures the annual percentage of the nominal that will be repaid by anticipation if the prepayment rate adheres to the month's SMM. The CPR is therefore an annualised SMM:

$$CPR = \left[1 - (1 - SMM)^{12}\right] \text{ and } SMM = 1 - (1 - CPR)^{1/12}$$

- PSA (Public Standard Association) is a standardised series of CPR which defines a reference curve h_t for discussion among professionals (traders, bankers...). The PSA curve assumes the following:

- linear growth of the CPRs from 0% to 6% over 30 months, i.e. +0.2% per month,
- followed by stability over the following months.

Convention allows the use of a single coefficient to roughly describe the prepayment speed of a pool. For example, 200 PSA means that the CPR doubles, passing from 0 to 12% in thirty months. The PSA curve is mainly used to calculate the prepayment rate of the American MBS and for discussion amongst traders. It is a model that is not generally adapted for RMBS modeling but as each institution usually keeps their model confidential, the method allows for a comparison of price from one single number.

Once the CPR(t) "average" curve has been defined, the majority of models use a coefficient $k(t, r_{i,t})$ in the same way as for the PSA. $k(.)$ is a function of time and the rates curve that expresses the variations in this CPR curve according to a rise in the interest rate.

Example of CPR settings in two temporal series: $h(t)$ x $coef(t, scenario\ i)$.

Description	St Dt	Dura	Expiration Date	Coupon	Coupo Type	Fixing Type	Coupor Basis	Freque	Tax	Attri	CPR	CDR
Mortgages fixed rate	223			0.05	Fixed	In Ad...	A30360	Mon...	N...	In...	coefRA*RA_Mortgages	cdR_mortgages
Mortgages fixed rate cst. pay	200			0.03937	Fixed	In Ad...	A30360	Mon...	N...	In...	coefRA*RA_Mortgages	cdR_mortgages
Mortgages fixed rate amort. cst.	228			0.02997	Fixed	In Ad...	A30360	Mon...	N...	In...	coefRA*RA_Mortgages	cdR_mortgages
Mortgages var. rate in fine	133			e3M	Floa...	In Ad...	ACT...	Mon...	N...	In...	coefRA*RA_Mortgages	cdR_mortgages
Mortgages var. rate cst. pay	245			e3M	Floa...	In Ad...	ACT...	Mon...	N...	In...	coefRA*RA_Mortgages	cdR_mortgages
Mortgages var. rate amort. cst.	330			e3M	Floa...	In Ad...	ACT...	Mon...	N...	In...	coefRA*RA_Mortgages	cdR_mortgages
TOTAL (€)												

This methodology has the great advantage of easily modeling a wave of prepayments in case of a move of the interest rates as well as a translation of the "average" curve.

Decision criteria for the client to exercise the repurchase option
A client prepaying because of interest rates will take the decision to exercise the repurchase option taking into consideration the new interest rates available on the market and his/her own rate. There are different possible ways of expressing its calculation:

- the difference in IR for the same market loan for the remaining duration,
- the difference in IR for a new loan with the same characteristics as his/her loan at inception,
- the marked to market profit that the client makes by exercising the option: at first approximation, the nominal multiplied by the modified duration multiplied by the difference in IR on the remaining duration,
- the marked to market profit as a percentage of the remaining nominal. In fact, the choice between these two last expressions lies in the ability to take into account the factor of scale in the client's decision: clients do not behave in the same manner according to the size of their due remaining capital, those with larger amounts tend to behave more rationally.

From there, the prepayment percentage during the time period dt becomes $S_t.h_t.dt$ and as the contracts draw closer to their maturity over time, h_s also tends to draw closer to zero. In the same manner, at 0, $h_0 = 0$.

The modeling of the function h_t has given place to numerous studies of which the principal difficulty lies primarily in the collection of data.

In their credit contract the client holds an American option C_t of the exercise price P_t that is variable in time and is similar to a bond option, more so than to a 'swaption', due to the fact the credit spread is included. In fact a loan is no more relative to a bond than to another legal form of receivable. The question of knowing when the client is interested in prepaying their loan is more complex than it appears to be. A first reaction is to consider that, as it can be renegotiated as many times as wished, they should exercise their option as soon as they generate a minimum profit that covers the operational costs plus a certain margin (this one being in a cox-ross model the intrinsic value above the remaining option value). In reality it is difficult to refinance a 20 year credit more than two or three times, that's called the exhaustion effect. In addition, in the same way that an institution that adds an anticipated repurchase clause to its bonds ('callable bonds') will not always exercise this clause as soon as it is profitable (that is as soon as the intrinsic value exceeds the time value), the institution will wait until the profit reaches a sufficient size before doing so. There is therefore an optimal repurchase date, depending on the client's anticipation regarding the movement of the rates, their own spread and the market depth (that provides the necessary liquidity for repayment). There are two types of models:

- In cases where the formula is path dependent, calculations are extremely complex. The most advanced theories enable the determination by estimation of this date according to the information available; they use stopping times mathematical theories on the Brownian movement and Snell envelopes. The difficulty remains that the estimation is already quite complex even, for example, in the model of Heath, Jarrow and Morton[5]. a relatively simple continuous model, with the advantage of being close to the objective required for a direct correlation with the rate curve. And it rarely takes into account the crossover effects of spreads and rates (on the client spread and that of the bank). Operationally, banks use Monte-Carlo simulations to solve these problems most of the time but the calibration of the model is challenging and pricing can get far away from market prices.

- For formula independent of the path, tree models provide a good estimate especially if well calibrated with the market volatility curve. These models are most of the time sufficient and the only loss is the "media effect", which can be compensated for independently.

Finally, if formally the price estimation of the option requires a calculation for each credit, it is generally simpler to group clients by subclass and by behavior.

Aggregated behaviors

As already expressed, the clients' behavior is not always rational. Rather, it depends more on the individual anticipations of each client and so is

---
[5] See Notions of Financial Mathematics

different for each of them. For credit organization, the clients appear to be renegotiating in a fairly random sense around the unknown optimum value, which can enable substantial profits. Certain clients for example almost never renegotiate the conditions of their contracts. The previously mentioned function h_t has the purpose of translating this phenomenon. According to the value of the option C_t, it describes the behavior of the client. The modeling there is very flexible even if it needs to obey to a certain number of existing constraints. In particular, h_t by definition is limited on $\mathcal{R}$ to [0.1], rising (the higher the value of the option, so more clients will decide to exercise it).

Moreover, for negative values of the intrinsic value, we can assume h to be constant, or at least independent of the value of C_t and equal to k_t, a real element of [0.1], eventually random itself and representing the structural prepayment rate (this is an approximation, one observes that in case of increase of the IR, customers tend to keep their loans at low coupon as much as possible and do some kind of arbitrage).

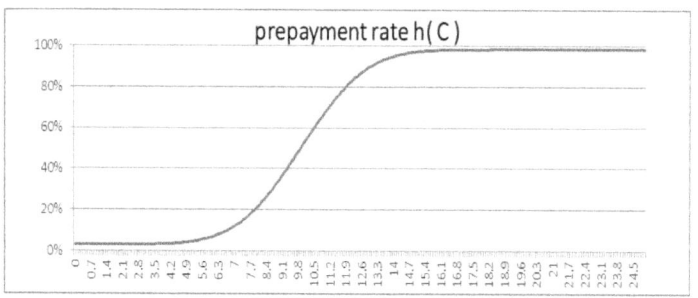

The key to the model lies in the fact that h_t depends on the rates through the intermediary of C_t or ($r_{market}(t)$-$r_{credit}(t)$) or the intrinsic value of the option ($r_{market}(t)$-$r_{credit}(t)$) * modified duration of the remaining loan(t). The choice between models indicating a direct or indirect dependence on the interest rates will be dictated by the necessary information and the model's simplicity.

h_t also depends on parameters that are exogenous but allow for the calibration of the model: The percentage of prepayments said to be uncompressible k_t, the clients' sensitivity to the valuation of their repurchase option, the efficiency of the network's persuasion concerning requests not to exercise the option... Also, as h_t depends on the clients' perception of the rate movements, in the same way, h_t depends on the past. Therefore, after a move in the interest rates, the prepayments generally first increase and then come down.

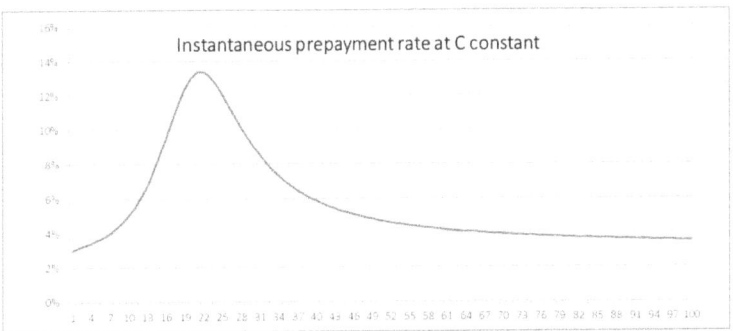

The number of clients deciding to exercise their option increases first and then decreases towards the incompressible rate. In fact, if after a certain amount of time, a client has not decided to exercise the repurchase option, it is most likely because he has not judged it advisable or anticipate a better period (in terms of being more micro-economic, the option's utility function does not justify the exercise). We could also model this by assuming that the prepayments, at constant C_t, depend on the past of C_t.

We can also use this compartmental specificity to just assume that when interest rates move down, clients willing to exercise will do so, leaving the pool with the remaining clients. This observation explains why non path-dependent trees pricing models are acceptable.

Choice of model
The choice of model depends on the data available. Most of the institutions we have worked with unfortunately do not keep enough data to develop sophisticated models.

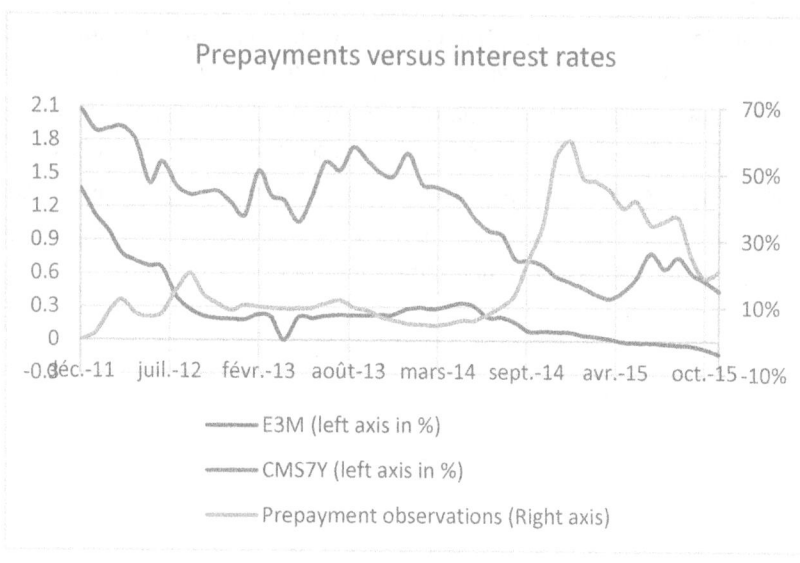

The portfolio we used for analysis presents high similarity with the whole Belgium market, for which the Belfius Bank portfolio is a good proxy considering its market share.

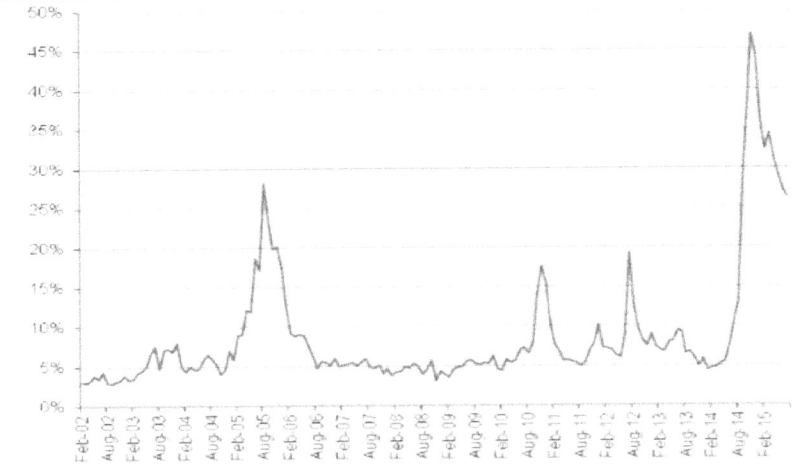

Source: Belfius Bank Originated Belgian Residential Mortgage Portfolio

We tested two models which do not integrate the initial coupon of the loans since this information was not available. By doing so, we consider indeed this coupon as integrated to the parameters. This may appear disappointing but actually, it was not since the whole pool was generated around the same time, giving a homogeneous behavior. During our period of observation unfortunately interest rates were stable or down, so we have not been able to really test the assumption of a minimum prepayment rate (the current environment will provide an answer this question over the next years...). Again, certain indications we received on other portfolios show that there is also an adaptation of prepayments if IR are increasing.

The first model considers the prepayment rate as proportional to the 3 months average move of the interest rate from inception.

$dCPR(t) = a \cdot dCMS7Y + b$

The resulting sensitivity is +25 pts of prepayments for -1 pts on the long-term interest rate on average. The statistical tests are good with R2 above 70% but still the pick observed when the decrease in IR amplified is not caught by the linear regression. However, it seems that there was a seasonality effect with people not reacting during summer and postponing to after their vacations (the average duration of a renegotiation is of about 2 to 3 months) which may explain the strong peak.

In both models, the **structural prepayments appear to be around 5 to 7 points** according to other observations on Belgium market. The French market is lower (2 to 5 pts). We call "structural prepayments", the prepayment rate observed when IR are stable, not when they are up.

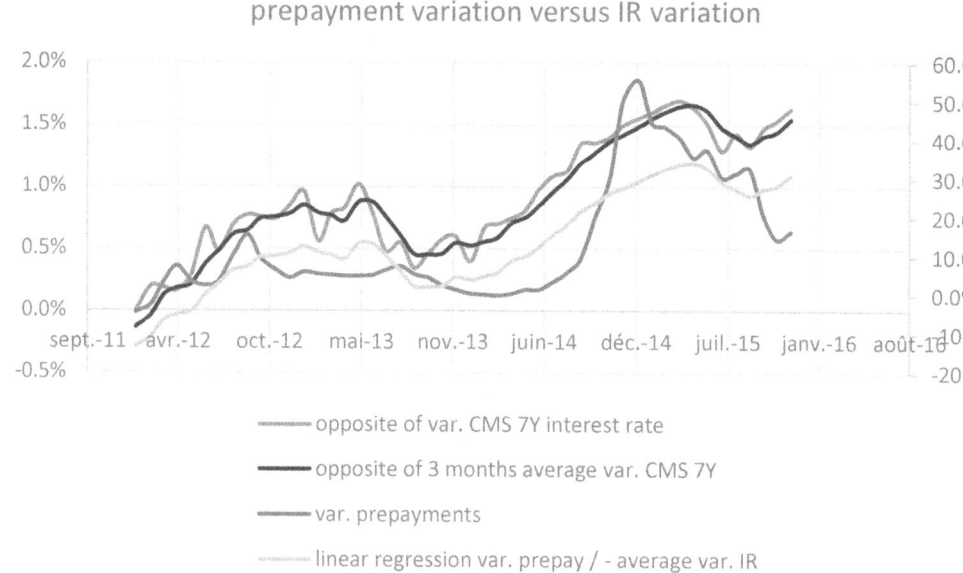

The second model takes into account the amplification effect when IR move is significant, by doing the regression of the prepayments on the square of the move of IR.

$$dCPR(t) = a.(dCMS7Y)^2 + b$$

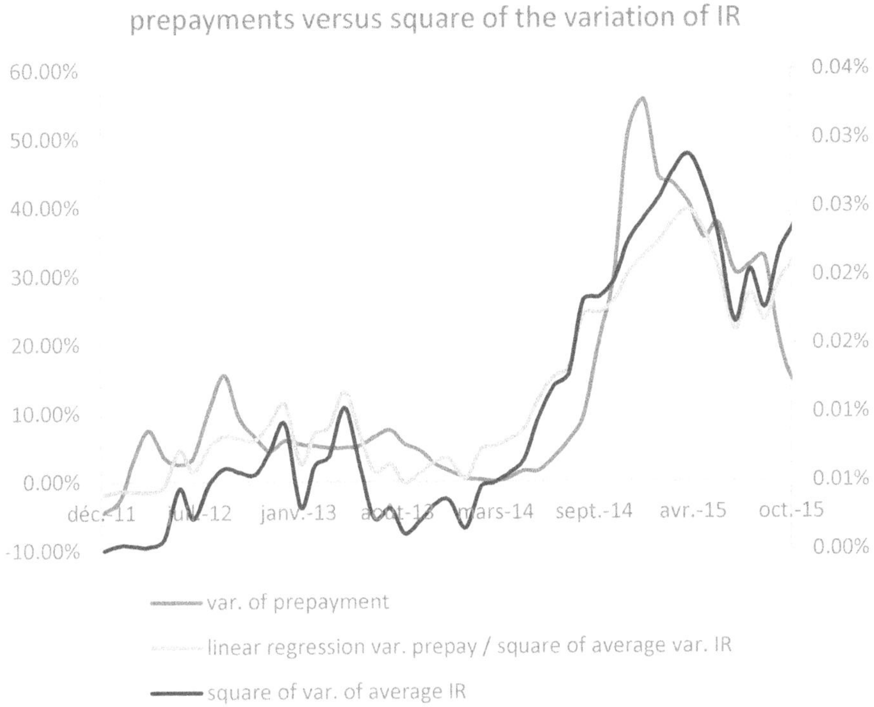

prepayments versus square of the variation of IR

— var. of prepayment
······ linear regression var. prepay / square of average var. IR
— square of var. of average IR

Results are better, they can be summarized in the following table:

Var. of IR	prepayments
-1%	7% + 15% = 22%
-2%	7% + 60% = 67%
-3%	90%

No statistics are available above 3%. The 3% move effect was observed on a part of the portfolio. All loans were renegotiated except 10% one year after the move.

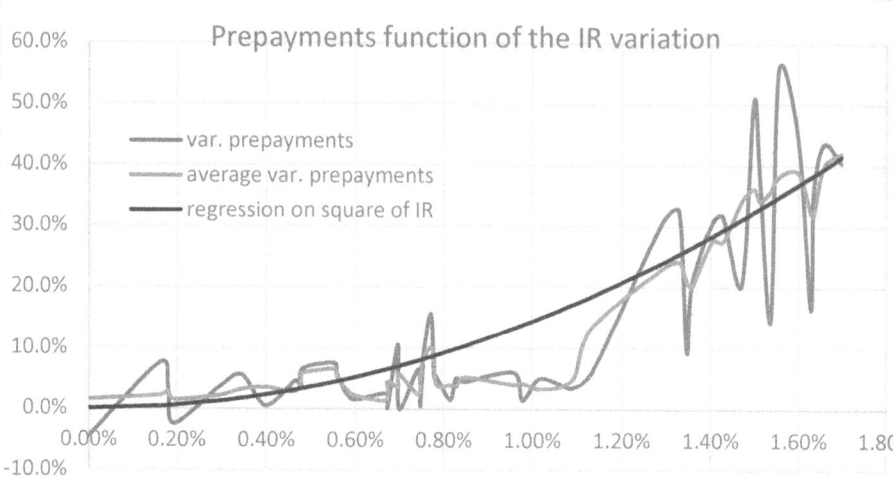

In addition, what we observed is that:

1. Customers seem to exercise their option depending on the IR variation independently of the remaining duration of their loan: indeed, they do not price the actualized value of their option but rather the amount of savings generated the first month. Modeling the percentage of prepayments function of the difference of IR is sufficient in the first approximation.
2. Customers exercise when their "strike level" is reached, fairly independently of the past path. The sophisticated path-dependent models do not seem to be mandatory considering the rough estimate that we are looking for and binomial pricings are absolutely acceptable.
3. There is a strong seasonality.
4. A wave of prepayments lasts between 3 to 12 months.

Subsequently, we suggest to use a simple model where the prepayment rate depends on the difference between market rates and loans rates:

Move of rate	Additional prepayments	Cumulative prepayments
+2% and above	-1%	3%
+1%	-1%	4%
0%	5%	5%
- 0.5%	5%	10%
- 1%	10%	20%
- 1.5%	20%	40%
- 2%	25%	65%
- 2.5%	20%	85%
- 3% and more	5%	90%

There is 5% of prepayments independent of the interest rates. We observe also a symmetric phenomenon under which, if interest rates are going up, this "independent" prepayment level goes down slightly: the customers seek a way to keep their mortgage if this way appears to be a cheap one.

In a pool that we studied, after an increase in 3% of the IR, the CPR was down around 2%.
After a move down of the long-term interest rates by 300 bps, the stock has been prepaid at 90%. The remaining 10% are supposed insensitive to IR.

The parameters of the table can be adjusted to different pools but the methodology remains the same. The choice of discretionary steps of 0.5% has the advantage of reducing the time of calculation for the pricing of the swaptions.

It is obvious that models with better data would generate more precise estimates but this global model is already capturing the key elements of risks faced by banks. ALM is not an exact science and does not have the goal to deliver accurate trading P&L. ALM must first avoid disasters as were observed during the 2008 crisis following massive errors.

Passage to the continuous model

It is interesting to complete this very pragmatic approach with a more theoretical view.

Modeling constant instantaneous reimbursements

The credits with constant monthly reimbursements are the essential part of a bank balance sheet at fixed rate for, as an example, the French banks. This is why it is interesting to undertake a short methodological digression in order to understand the impact of prepayments via continuous time. The passage to continuous also enables a simple analysis[6] of the stock effects on a balance sheet and calculations relative to sensitivity.

If we use the example of a credit pool with constant prepayments, for an initial duration T, an interest rate of r and the initial nominal $CRD(0) = 1$. We have a trivial $CRD(T) = 0$.

Exclusive of anticipated repayments, we therefore have the immediate reimbursement rate at $t\ m.dt$ corresponding to:
- the repayment of the principal: $-dCRD(t)$
- and the interest payments $r.CRD(t).dt$

That is:
$$m.dt = -dCRD(t) + r.CRD(t).dt$$
The solution of this differential equation is in the following form:

$$CRD(t) = \left(1 - \frac{m}{r}\right).e^{r.t} + \frac{m}{r} \text{ in order to satisfy } CRD(0)=1$$

The constraint at expiry of $CRD(T)=0$ implies
$$m = \frac{r}{1 - e^{-r.T}}$$

And
$$CRD(t) = \frac{1 - e^{-r.(T-t)}}{1 - e^{-r.T}}$$

$$dCRD(t) = \frac{-r.e^{-r.(T-t)}}{1 - e^{-r.T}}.dt$$

$$\frac{dCRD(t)}{CRD(t)} = \frac{-r.e^{-r.(T-t)}}{1 - e^{-r.(T-t)}}.dt$$

The credit price at moment t for an instantaneous rate of x is worth:

---

[6] For a bank that produces constant monthly credits every day for an initial duration of 15 years for example, the continuous modeling will not be bad if the market rates remain stable.

$$P(t,x) = m.\int_t^T e^{-x.u}.du = m.\frac{e^{-x.t}-e^{-x.T}}{x} = \frac{r}{x}.\frac{e^{-x.t}-e^{-x.T}}{1-e^{-r.T}}$$

And the modified duration:

More specifically:
$$-\frac{\partial \ln P(t,x)}{\partial x} = \frac{1}{x} - \frac{T.e^{-x.T}-t.e^{-x.t}}{e^{-x.t}-e^{-x.T}}$$

$$-\frac{\partial \ln P(t=0,x=r)}{\partial x} = \frac{1}{r} - \frac{T}{e^{r.T}-1}$$

Rate sensitivity for a constant monthly payments credit, no prepayments.

duration / rate	0%	3%	5%	10%
5	2.5	2.4	2.4	2.3
10	5.0	4.8	4.6	4.2
15	7.5	6.9	6.6	5.7
20	10.0	9.0	8.4	6.9
25	12.4	11.0	10.0	7.8

The expressions have the great advantage of enabling very simple calculations.

Modeling a stock of loans

A bank actually produces loans every day and its stock is the sum of these different loans. If one wants to model simply the stock of loans, one has to see the impact of this addition of different loans with different maturities. For constant reimbursements loans, the result is extremely simple. Indeed, for a constant instantaneous rate r, the stock at t of a bank producing 1 at each moment u is constant:

$$stock(t) = \int_{t-T}^{t} CRD(t, \text{ expiring date } u+T).du = \int_{t-T}^{t} \frac{1-e^{-r.(T+u-t)}}{1-e^{-r.T}}.du$$

$$stock(t) = \int_{0}^{T} \frac{1-e^{-r.v}}{1-e^{-r.T}}.dv \text{ with } v = T+u-t$$

$$stock = \frac{T}{1-e^{-r.T}} - \frac{1}{r}$$

The stock is not only constant but also equals to the modified duration of the initial loans.

However, this interesting result doesn't allow to avoid modelling each vintage separately. Indeed, one must keep in mind that the effects of a move of the interest rate on the stock are always progressive in their distribution, which a global modelling would not express.

Therefore, the expressed derivative always gives the stock "market priced" sensitivity at a variation of the rate but this will not impact entirely the stock before its complete renewal, which is after a duration of T (out of prepayment effect which shorten the renewal of the stock).

Integrating prepayments

Let us now suppose an anticipated prepayment rate $h(t).CRD(t).dt$ of t, the equation on the capital amortisation will be modified due to this supplementary parameter which will impact the nominal on the instantaneous payments. The capital variation remaining of $CRD(t)$ comes from normal reimbursements on the remaining nominal, that is taking into account the past prepayments (which reduce the monthly payment in proportion) and instantaneous prepayments. The prepayments reduce the monthly reimbursement in proportion of the initial nominal prepaid, that means that the new monthly payments become $m.e^{-\int_{0}^{t} h(u).du}$ and consequently the variation of CRD is coming from the normal reimbursements plus the prepayments:

$$-dCRD(t) = m.e^{-\int_0^t h(u).du}.dt - r.CRD(t) + h.CRD(t).dt$$

$$-dCRD(t) = m.e^{-\int_0^t h(u).du}.dt + (h-r).CRD(t).dt$$

The equation is very similar to the previous one which was the solution of:
$$m.dt = -dCRD_{h=0}(t) + r.CRD_{h=0}(t).dt$$

Let write $CRD(t,h) = CRD_{h=0}(t).e^{-\int_0^t h(u).du}$

Then

$$dCRD(t,h) = dCRD_{h=0}(t).e^{-\int_0^t h(u).du} - h(t).e^{-\int_0^t h(u).du}.CRD_{h=0}(t).dt$$

$$dCRD(t,h) = -m.e^{-\int_0^t h(u).du} + [r - h(t)]e^{-\int_0^t h(u).du}.CRD_{h=0}(t).dt$$

$$-dCRD(t,h) = m.e^{-\int_0^t h(u).du} + [h(t) - r].CRD(t,h).dt$$

Therefore, one have: $CRD(t) = \dfrac{1-e^{-r(T-t)}}{1-e^{-r.T}}.e^{-\int_0^t h(u).du}$

The formula replicates the expression excluding anticipated prepayments multiplied by the survival function.

Profile of an amortization on a 20 year constant monthly credit according to a prepayment rate.

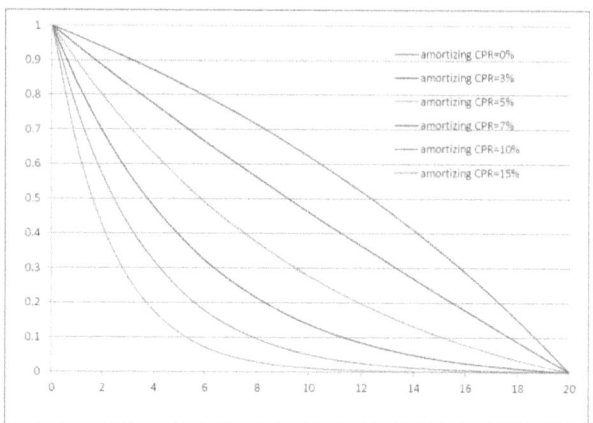

For h constant, one gets:

$$CRD(t) = \frac{1-e^{-r(T-t)}}{1-e^{-rT}} \cdot e^{-ht}$$

$$dCRD(t) = \frac{-h-(r-h)e^{-r(T-t)}}{1-e^{-rT}} \cdot e^{-ht} \cdot dt - t \cdot \frac{1-e^{-r(T-t)}}{1-e^{-rT}} \cdot e^{-ht} \cdot dh + \frac{(T-t) \cdot e^{-r(T-t)} + t \cdot e^{-r(2T-t)} - T \cdot e^{-rT}}{\left(1-e^{-rT}\right)^2} \cdot e^{-ht} \cdot dr$$

$$\frac{dCRD(t)}{CRD(t)} = \frac{-h-(r-h)e^{-r(T-t)}}{1-e^{-r(T-t)}} \cdot dt - t \cdot dh + \frac{(T-t) \cdot e^{-r(T-t)} + t \cdot e^{-r(2T-t)} - T \cdot e^{-rT}}{\left(1-e^{-rT}\right) \cdot \left(1-e^{-r(T-t)}\right)} \cdot dr$$

The credit price at moment t for an instantaneous market rate of x is worth:

$$P(t,x,h) = \int_t^T \left[m \cdot e^{-hu} + h \cdot CRD(u) \right] \cdot e^{-xu} \cdot du$$

$$P(t,x,h) = m \cdot \frac{e^{-(x+h)t} - e^{-(x+h)T}}{x+h} + \frac{h \cdot m}{r} \cdot \int_t^T \left(e^{-(h+x)u} - e^{-rT+(r-h-x)u} \right) \cdot du$$

$$P(t,x,h) = \frac{r}{x+h} \cdot \frac{e^{-(x+h)t} - e^{-(x+h)T}}{1-e^{-rT}} + \frac{h}{1-e^{-rT}} \cdot \left[\frac{e^{-(h+x)t} - e^{-(h+x)T}}{h+x} - e^{-rT} \cdot \frac{e^{(r-h-x)T} - e^{(r-h-x)t}}{r-h-x} \right]$$

$$P(t,x,h) = \frac{e^{-(x+h)t} - e^{-(x+h)T}}{1-e^{-rT}} \cdot \frac{r+h}{x+h} - \frac{h}{r-h-x} \cdot \frac{e^{(r-h-x)T} - e^{(r-h-x)t}}{e^{rT}-1}$$

The formula provides the price of a path-through RMBS in our simple model and the sensitivity of the price to a move of the parameters h, t or x.

$$P(t, x=r+dx, h) = \frac{e^{-(r+dx+h)t} - e^{-(r+dx+h)T}}{1-e^{-rT}} \cdot \frac{r+h}{r+dx+h} + \frac{h}{h+dx} \cdot \frac{e^{-(h+dx)T} - e^{-(h+dx)t}}{e^{rT}-1}$$

$$P(t=0, x=r+dx, h) = \frac{e^{rT} - e^{-(dx+h)T}}{e^{rT}-1} \cdot \frac{r+h}{r+dx+h} + \frac{h}{h+dx} \cdot \frac{e^{-(h+dx)T}-1}{e^{rT}-1}$$

With a limited development of degree one, one gets:

$$P(t=0, x=r+dx, h) = 1 - \frac{dx}{e^{rT}-1} \cdot \left[\frac{e^{rT} - e^{-hT}}{r+h} + \frac{e^{-hT}-1}{h} \right] + o(dx)$$

We get back the previous formula for h small:

$$P(t=0, x=r+dx, h \approx 0) = 1 - dx \cdot \left[\frac{1}{r} - \frac{T}{e^{rT}-1} \right] + o(dx)$$

The formula provides the impact of the prepayment on the modified duration of the price. Notice that the same methodology gives the sensitivity of the price to a variation of h.

Notice that at origin, by construction, $P(t=0, x=r, h) = 1$. A variation of anticipated h just after issuing the RMBS does not impact its price because our implied 0-coupon curve is flat and investors are neutral in term of duration of their investments.

However, in reality, we see that moves of x and h are correlated.

Let write for small variations dx: $dh = \beta.dx$ (that is our first model) then:

$$P''(t=0, x=r+dx, h+\beta.dx) = \frac{e^{rT} - e^{-hT-(1+\beta)T.dx}}{e^{rT}-1} \cdot \frac{r+h+\beta.dx}{r+h+(1+\beta).dx} + \frac{h+\beta.dx}{h+(1+\beta).dx} \cdot \frac{e^{-hT-(1+\beta)T.dx}-1}{e^{rT}-1}$$

The formula above no longer expresses the price since it is not probabilistic (so the notation). Still it shows the mechanism of the duration extension effect on the actualized value of cash flows. However, this regards small variations whereas as ALM managers we are more interested in major ones.

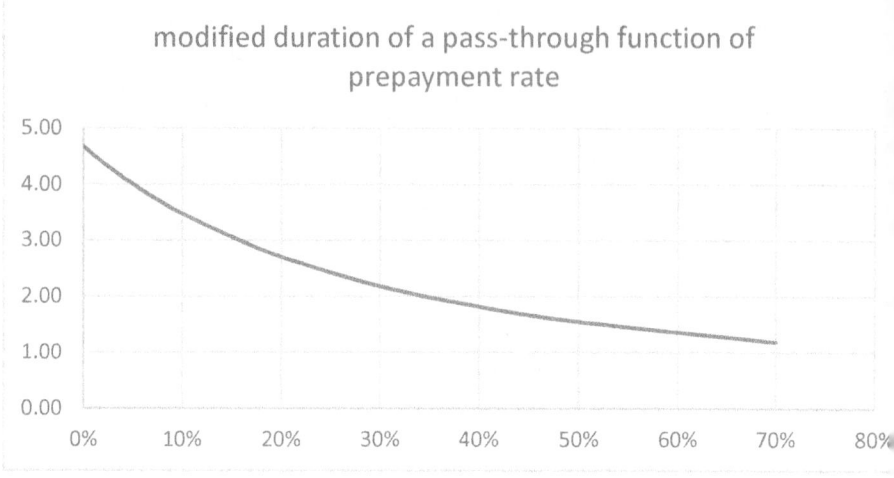

dx	-2.0%	-1.0%	0.0%	1.0%	2.0%
x	2.0%	3.0%	4.0%	5.0%	6.0%
r	4.0%	4.0%	4.0%	4.0%	4.0%
h	40.0%	20.0%	5.0%	4.0%	3.0%
T	10	10	10	10	10
Price	103.77%	102.77%	100.00%	96.00%	92.00%
Price if h cst = 5%	108.50%	104.12%	100.00%	96.12%	92.45%

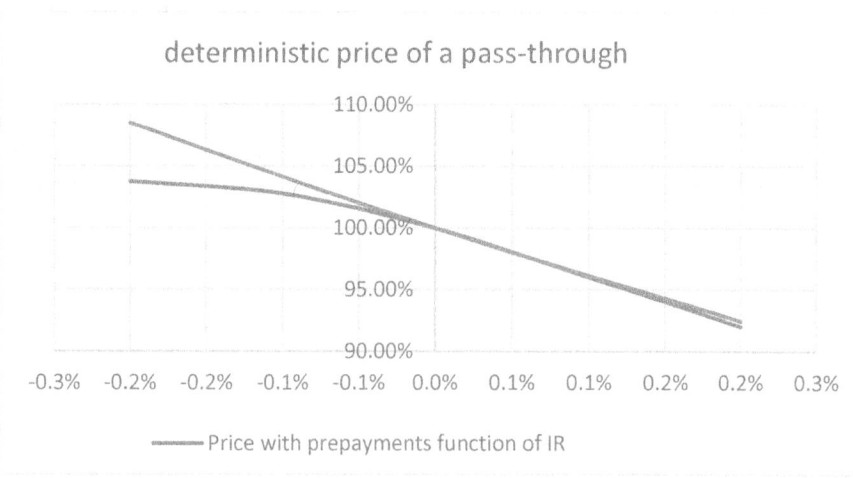

This methodology of pricing assumes an automatic linear sensitivity of the instantaneous prepayment rate to a variation in interest rates but does not include the uncertainty in the variation of interest rates. In a probabilistic environment, the value of the bond becomes the expected value of this set of cash flows under the risk neutral probability. In a simple model where x is a random variable, one gets:

$$P(t,x) = E\tilde{P}(t=0, x = r+dx, h+\beta.dx) = E\left[\frac{e^{r.T} - e^{-h.T-(1+\beta).T.dx}}{e^{r.T}-1} \cdot \frac{r+h+\beta.dx}{r+h+(1+\beta).dx} + \frac{h+\beta.dx}{h+(1+\beta).dx} \cdot \frac{e^{-h.T-(1+\beta).T.dx}-1}{e^{r.T}-1}\right]$$

Modeling a stock of loans with prepayments

A regular production of loans with same characteristics generates also a constant stock:

$$stock(t) = \int_{t-T}^{t} CRD(t, \text{ expiring date } u+T).du = \int_{t-T}^{t} \frac{1-e^{-r.(T+u-t)}}{1-e^{-r.T}} . e^{-\int_{u}^{t} h(v).dv} .du$$

$$stock(t) = \int_{0}^{T} \frac{1-e^{-r.v}}{1-e^{-r.T}} . e^{-h.(T-v)} dv \text{ with } v = T+u-t \text{ et } h \text{ constant}$$

$$stock = \frac{e^{-h.T}}{1-e^{-r.T}} \cdot \left[\frac{e^{h.v}}{h} + \frac{e^{-(h+r)v}}{h+r}\right]_{0}^{T} = \frac{e^{-h.T}}{1-e^{-r.T}} \cdot \left[\frac{e^{h.T}-1}{h} - \frac{1-e^{-(h+r)T}}{h+r}\right]$$

Pricing the option

Theoretical considerations

To summarize, the American option the bank sold becomes the possibility of paying, at any time, the wealth Z_t as follows:

$$Z_t = h_t.C_t.e^{-\int_{0}^{t} h_u.du}$$

In this way, the problem becomes a classic exercise (although complex) of *pricing* that modern pricing tools can resolve. One should note however that the price also depends on the underlying volatility (as the clients display a period of latency before reacting, the short volatility is therefore not appropriate).

As h_t increases with C_t, we obtain a continuum of emerging options: The more expensive the option, the higher the number of clients that repurchase their credit. In technical terms, the sensitivity (or modified duration) of a credit pool is variable: by convexity we mean the second derivation of price[7]. The credits are of a negative convexity:

- The more rates decrease, the more the clients prepay and the more the credits pool (or the MBS) duration decreases. It is clear that the discount factors of cash flows appreciate but as these cash flows decrease in their duration, the price increases less than with a vanilla bond of a weak (and negative) convexity.

- Conversely, the more the rates increase, the less the clients prepay and the longer the credit pool duration becomes at the time when the discount factors depreciate. Therefore its price decreases faster than with a standard bond.

IR	Bond in fine		Pool of linear amortizing loans (over 12 years)		
	price	Modified duration	Price	Modified duration	CPR
1%	119,4%	4,544	115,30%	3,77	15,0%
2%	114,1%	4,489	111,94%	3,92	12,5%
3%	109,2%	4,435	108,4%	4,15	9,5%
4%	104,5%	4,382	104,4%	4,33	7,0%
5%	100,0%	4,329	100%	4,47	5,0%
6%	95,8%	4,278	95,56%	4,47	4,0%
7%	91,8%	4,227	91,31%	4,41	3,5%
8%	88,0%	4,177	87,34%	4,32	3,3%
9%	84,4%	4,128	83,64%	4,21	3,1%
10%	81,0%	4,080	80,17%	4,11	3,0%

The pricing of the negative convexity is expressed via the spread that an RMBS pays in relation to a standard bond of the same sensitivity. It is in fact an interesting way of defining the cost of a prepayment option for the internal transfer rate (see related chapter).

---

[7] See "Notions of financial mathematics", 1.1.7.1 page 34:

$$c = \frac{1}{P} \cdot \frac{\partial^2 P}{\partial r^2} \text{ and } P(r+dr) = P(r) \cdot \left[1 - s.dr + \frac{c}{2}.dr^2 + o(dr^2) \right]$$

The banks generally cover themselves against negative convexity by purchasing 'swaptions' in such a way that their NBI global variations remain within the limits they have fixed. The operations are therefore placed in macro-hedging and the internal transfer rates are generally impacted as a pro-rata of the option premiums paid. There again, the superiority of a global modelling method of the balance sheet (therefore with the new production) is incontestable. In fact, if for example during a period of rising rates, there is a lack of profit with the stock, the new production is, itself, generally favoured by the economic growth climate (the rates rise due to the anticipated inflation): The retail banks are normally favoured by a rise in the long term rates (as their retail resources are not very sensitive to interest rates in general). However, the market banks need to be far more attentive to this phenomenon due to their variable refinancing rate (they generally lend for this at variable rates).

It should be noted that the covering strategies based on swaptions are incomplete if they do not completely integrate the correlation between the issuer's spread and that of the clients (or the retail client margin): In a period of recession, the rates decrease, the clients repay faster, production slows and often, due to competition, the client margins decrease[8] (at least at the beginning of the crisis). This effect reduces the NBI of the bank at the time when its own spread may rise due to the recession and therefore increases the cost of its market resources (as it was observed during the last crisis). In parallel, recession may lead to an increase in risk (but not always).

Modeling example taking into account the CPR and CDR

---

[8] The effect of decreasing margins due to the decrease in volumes can be observed mainly on the good quality retail files. It was balanced during the crisis of 2008 by a general rise in the spreads and the crunch of banking capacities. The phenomenon is therefore difficult to predict as it really depends on the global economic context.

Model Analysis: A00145

	0	1	2	3	4	5	6	7	8	9
Interest Rate	3.94 %	3.94 %	3.94 %	3.94 %	3.94 %	3.94 %	3.94 %	3.94 %	3.94 %	3.94 %
Current Nominal	400,000.00	395,597.33	389,844.14	384,164.19	378,556.63	373,019.98	367,551.91	363,362.72	359,211.95	35
Theorical Face	400,000.00	400,000.00	398,572.04	397,139.39	395,702.04	394,259.98	392,813.18	391,361.64	389,905.34	38
Default	0.00	124.00	124.94	124.10	123.25	123.03	124.34	122.52	121.12	
Standard Reimbursement	0.00	0.00	1,411.80	1,400.83	1,389.94	1,379.13	1,368.40	1,357.74	1,351.67	
Prepayments	0.00	4,278.67	4,216.45	4,155.02	4,094.37	4,034.48	3,975.34	2,708.93	2,677.99	
Recovery (with lag)	0.00	80.60	81.21	80.67	80.11	79.97	80.82	79.64	78.73	
Losses / Impairments	0.00	-43.40	-43.73	-43.44	-43.14	-43.06	-43.52	-42.88	-42.39	
CPR	12.84 %	12.84 %	12.84 %	12.84 %	12.84 %	12.84 %	8.88 %	8.88 %	8.88 %	
CDR	0.37 %	0.38 %	0.38 %	0.39 %	0.39 %	0.40 %	0.40 %	0.40 %	0.40 %	
LGD	35.00 %	35.00 %	35.00 %	35.00 %	35.00 %	35.00 %	35.00 %	35.00 %	35.00 %	
Cumulative Delinquencie...	0.00 %	0.03 %	0.06 %	0.09 %	0.12 %	0.15 %	0.19 %	0.22 %	0.25 %	
Cumulative Losses (on i...	0.00 %	0.01 %	0.02 %	0.03 %	0.04 %	0.05 %	0.07 %	0.08 %	0.09 %	
Cumulative CPR (on initi...	0.00 %	1.07 %	2.12 %	3.16 %	4.19 %	5.19 %	6.19 %	6.87 %	7.54 %	

Having said that, banks are structural options sellers, in the same way that they are structural liquidity transformers. Entirely covering this risk would make no sense, even more so as it should be analysed as an element in the global balance sheet deviation. Finally, as clients are not perfectly informed and trained to understand options theories, their exercising of the option continue to exhibit un-optimised behavior which is to the benefit of the bank.

Operational pricing

The usual methodology used by banks is based on Monte-Carlo simulations calibrated using market parameters. However, these approaches present some disadvantages:

- Pricing are rough estimates, not taking into account all market parameters,
- Models are complex and heavy to implement,
- Models rarely provide a hedging strategy composed of vanilla market instruments.

We propose here a pragmatic solution to get a real "market" estimate of the price of this lapse option. Indeed, our approach is a mix of actuarial and investment bank techniques.

On the investment bank side, the source of the model will be market prices of vanilla interest rate instruments (swaps and options). These prices will then be used to calibrate the various models used. This calibration process ensures that the prices are accurate and that a hedging strategy can naturally be proposed by shifting the source instruments and looking at the impact on the global structure's present value.

We are trying here to model this product from different points of views:

- first from a pure banking perspective
- then from the perspective of the customer

The integration of the customers' behavior implies the modeling of their decision to exercising their option as described above. If we do not have sufficient historical data to calibrate precisely this behavior, our pricing methodology is simple enough to get prices for a range of lapse tables, giving us an indication of the impact of an error on the statistical description of customer behaviors.

The Models and their Calibration

Interest Rate Curve

For the analysis of the structure, we take a reinvestment assumption of Libor 3M, which is the standard of the market.

The model of IR is our market model used for all our capital market operations. It is fairly complex, but similar to the best practices used by major investment banks. As it is not the main driver of the structure's present value, we will not detail it. The Inputs are the bullet swaps of the interbank market (OIS, Euribor, FRAs ...) and the curve is modelled taking into account the exact dates for the ECB meeting and the specificities of the Euribor/Libor market (end of years...). We are using market data up to 50 years in order to cope with the very long durations observed in the portfolio.

Interest Rate options

We do use here the standard of the interbank market ZABR (or shifted SABR) model in order to calibrate the volatility cube.

The SABR Equations are:

$$dF_t = \sigma_t . F_t^\beta . dW_t$$
$$d\sigma_t = \alpha . \sigma_t . dZ_t$$
$$dZ_t . dW_t = \rho . dt$$

Because we are in a very low, even negative rate environment, the stochastic variable F above cannot be negative when $Beta > 0$, so it will not represent the rate but the shifted rate: $R + S$. The standard market practice is to take $S = 1\%$, thus allowing rates to go up to minus 1%. The resulting model is called ZABR.

There are four parameters in this model:

    i)   Sigma σ: this is the At The Money (ATM) volatility

ii) Beta β: is a parameter that allows to move between a Lognormal model(Beta=1) and a Normal model (Beta=0)
iii) The volatility sigma is stochastic and Alpha α is the volatility (Lognormal) of Sigma
iv) The two wiener processes dZ_t and dW_t, do have a correlation Rho ρ.

In practice, the Beta coefficient is set to a consensus value: between 20% and 40% for Euro.

We are then left with three parameters:

i) Sigma: ATM volatility
ii) Alpha or vovol: the volatility of the vol., this is linked to the strangle price
iii) Rho: if rates go up, does the vol. go up or down: correlation vol/rates, this is linked to the collar price.

So when looking at this problem, let us assume that one knows from the market the prices of the ATM straddle, a strangle 200 wide and a collar 200 wide. There are a total of three different strikes here: ATM, ATM+100 and ATM-100, for three unknowns giving an easy resolution.

However, this is not a linear system, but as always in finance the ZABR function is convex, the gradient algorithm can then safely be used to determine the values of sigma, rho and vovol.

Please note that our inputs here are three prices straddle, strangle and collar, but the same thing can be done with any three different strikes.

Once calibrated, the ZABR model formula produces a log vol that can be plugged into the classic Black Scholes formula in order to get the option price. The goal of all this process is to have a correct smile and accurate prices for all the strikes, this is very important as a simple log or normal model would produce prices very different from the market tradable prices. Indeed, standard simulation used in Monte-Carlo with lower quality of smile calibration can generate significantly different prices, some massively wrong. In the current market environment, we found that prices can be three times more expensive with a real market model than with a Monte-Carlo simulation.

Market information

From the Market price, using At The Money and Out of the Money option prices observed on the market, we build a global volatility cube, allowing to price any Swaption for any strike using the ZABR (shifted SABR) model.

In our calibration, around 100 prices are taken from the market and the parameters of ZABR are calibrated to match the inputs. We do allow for negative rates: our random variable is not the 5Y rate for example, but the (5Y plus 1%), thus 5Y rate can go up to -0.99%.

Forwards modeling: HJM Model

The Present Value of the position has been priced using HJM model with Mean Reversion.

Here are the equations of the Model:

$$df(t,T) = \mu(t,T).dt + \xi(t,T).dW(t)$$

and

$$\frac{dP(t,T)}{P(t,T)} = \left[r(t) - \alpha(t,T).\theta(t) \right].dt + \alpha(t,T).dW_t$$

In practice, in order to integrate the forwards into the option model, the model is implemented into a trinomial Tree similar to this one:

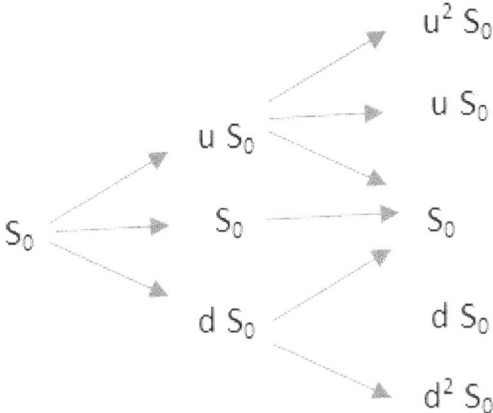

The variable modeled in the Tree is the instantaneous overnight rate, and knowing this rate, for each point of the tree, one can deduct the full yield curve.

We use this model in a simplified version: the mean reversion θ(t) will be taken as a constant, typically 1% / 3% will generate a decent Bid/Offer for the studied structure.

For the HJM volatility, ξ(t,T) will be taken as a step function between the calibration points:

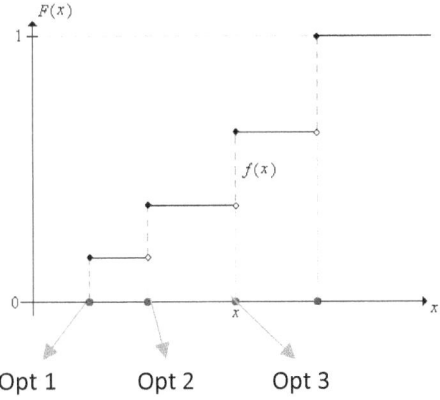

In the HJM Tree, all options prices with a maturity before Opt1 depend only from the HJM first volatility. Thus having an option with maturity Opt1 allows to determine the HJM Vol1.

Once the first Vol is set, the price of an option maturing at Opt2 will depend only on the HJM Vol2. The same principle is true for Opt3 and HJM Vol3.

This is a process very similar to the classic stripping of a yield curve, but applied here to options.

Obviously, one will need to carefully select the Swaptions and their strikes for the calibration.

Practical implementation of the Bermudian

A Bermudian option is the option to enter into a swap at regular dates (you can exercise the option only once). For example a Bermudian 10Y annual Payer 4% allows the buyer to enter in:

> 1Y into 9Y swap
>
> 2Y into 8Y swap
>
> ...
>
> 9Y into 1Y swap

Once the mean reversion parameter is set, a first calibration process will occur to build the volatility curve of HJM, this curve will be fitted to reprice exactly all the market prices of the underlying Swaptions, using the strike of the underlying swap. Here the choice of the calibrating instruments is pretty obvious.

Then similarly to the pricing of American options into Cox-Ross, the trinomial Tree is build, the final nodes are initialized at their intrinsic values and we move backward from the end of the tree towards today.

At each node where an exercise of swaption is possible, like 8Y where you can enter into a 2Y 4% payer swap, the following test is made:

```
// if it is a date where one can exercise and if intrinsic values is
superior to the remaining bermudian value, one exercises:
```

```
                int     swaptionInd   =   step->tree->bermudianOpt-
>getSwaptionIndex(stpInd);
                if(swaptionInd>=0)
                {
                        // calculate intrinsic value of the option
                        HullSwap  *underlying  =  &(this->step->tree-
>bermudianOpt->underlyingSwaps[swaptionInd]);
                        string type = this->step->tree->bermudianOpt-
>optType;
                        double     strike      =      this->step->tree-
>bermudianOpt->optStrike;
                        double under;
                        double intrVal = 0.0;

                        under = underlying->fxRate(hullCurve(), t, rt,
deltat, sigma);
                        if(type[0] == 'R' || type[0] == 'r')
                                intrVal = strike - under;        //
receiving
                        else
                                intrVal = under - strike;        //
paying

                        if(step->tree->accreting)
                                intrVal  *=  pow(1+strike,tStarted);
        // nono to get applied accreting  if so

                        intrVal *= underlying->level(hullCurve(), t,
rt, deltat, sigma);


                        if(intrVal<0)intrVal = 0;

                        // replacement of the node value coming from
the 3 following nodes by the intrinsic value of the swaption
                        // please note that the exercise is not made
when intrVal>0 but when IntrVal>bermudVal
                        // thus the real exercise point is ABOVE the
strike (for a payer)
                        if(intrVal>bermudVal)bermudVal = intrVal;
                }
                return bermudVal;
```

In this extract of our C++ code, the highlighted line corresponds to the optimum exercise of the Swaption, the future value of the Bermudian, being lower than the intrinsic value is discarded and replaced by the intrinsic value of the exercised option. This algorithm ensures that there is a maximum of one exercise: in an exercise node, all the right side of the Tree is discarded, being replaced by the intrinsic value of the swap.

Our first pricing is based indeed on Bermudian Swaptions. Subscribers are deemed to be optimal, they will exercise their options at the perfect time. The price therefore overestimates the real cost of prepayments option.

Pricing the real option
The previous model reflects the way that a Bank will price such a structure. If customers were finance professionals, they would be effectively optimal in the exercise of the option. Unfortunately, this does not reflect the behavior of individuals, they will NOT be optimal and far from it.

So we suggest to keep our actuarial approach of pricing, therefore we have to price this structure where:

- 5% of the clients will exercise when 50 bp in the money or more
- 10% 100 bp
- 20% 150 bp
- 25% 200 bp
- 20% 250 bp
- 5% 300 bp
- 10% will never exercise or exercise too early (not priced, but it should compensate)

Please note that the percentages and trigger levels above can be easily changed.

Then the problem is to price a bermudian option to pay X% **when rates are above X%+Trigger%.**

In the code above, the only change would be as follow:

```
if(under>strike+trigger){
    intrVal = trigger * underlying-
            >level(hullCurve(), t, rt, deltat,
            sigma);
    bermudVal = intrVal;
}
```

In economic terms, it means that the borrower will go for a more attractive loan when new rates are below his current rate minus the trigger.

We have now to price 6 options instead of one, but we will be much more accurate, our previous calibration process can be reused identically.

Results

The reality of behavior of the pool is described in the table we built on data observations:

Move of rate	CPR move	Cumulative CPR	Duration of the wave (months)	Cumulative additional prepayments in the wave compared to 0%
+2% and above	-1%	3%	12	-1%
+1%	-1%	4%	12	-1%
0%	5%	5%		
- 0.5%	5%	10%	12	5%
- 1%	10%	20%	12	15%
- 1.5%	20%	40%	12	35%
- 2%	25%	65%	12	60%
- 2.5%	20%	85%	12	80%
- 3% and more	5%	90%	12	85%

We have assumed a duration of 12 months for the customers to exercise their option. In reality, if the market goes up and then down, customers have no time to exercise their repurchase option. Volatility of the IR has indeed to be taken into account: the option the customers get is rather on the average of the interest rates over 3 months than on instantaneous IR.

Let us take the example of a pool of mortgages loans, constant monthly repayment, generated on an interest curve equal to the actual one plus 300 bps (because an example with the current one would not make real sense).

We then create 4 scenarios and their CPR curve (variable CPRloans below, the variable "wave" is equal to 1 during 12 month and then 0 in order to describe the wave of CPR following the IR decrease):

scenario	CPR	Cumulative CPR after 1 year
Current forward curve + 300 bp	5%	4.77%
Current forward curve + 200 bp	5% + 15% the first year	17.83%
Current forward curve + 100 bp	5% + 60% the first year	47.66%
Current forward curve	5% + 85% the first year	59.48%

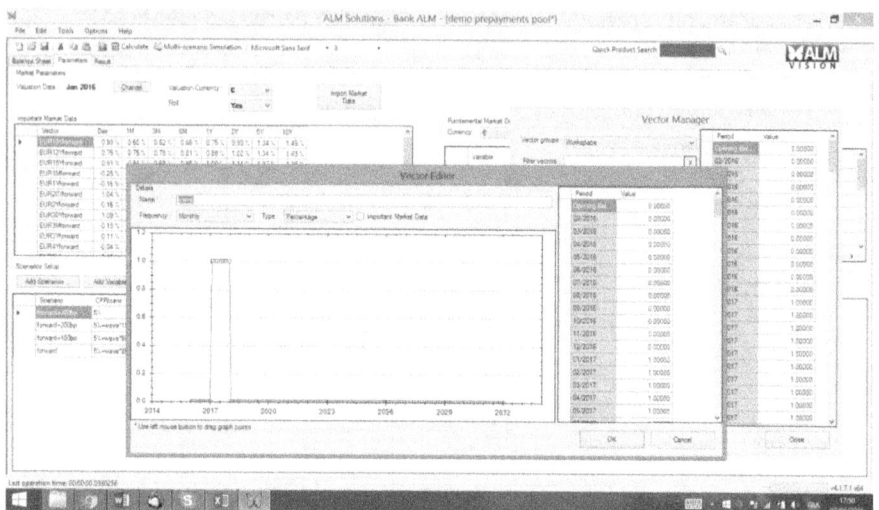

Amortization is obviously strongly impacted by the CPR:

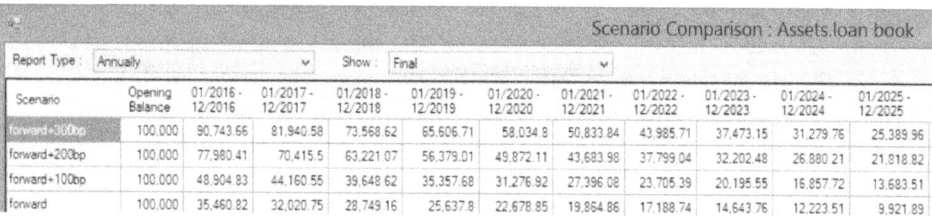

Scenario	Opening Balance	01/2016 - 12/2016	01/2017 - 12/2017	01/2018 - 12/2018	01/2019 - 12/2019	01/2020 - 12/2020	01/2021 - 12/2021	01/2022 - 12/2022	01/2023 - 12/2023	01/2024 - 12/2024	01/2025 - 12/2025
forward+300bp	100,000	90,743.66	81,940.58	73,568.62	65,606.71	58,034.8	50,833.84	43,985.71	37,473.15	31,279.76	25,389.96
forward+200bp	100,000	77,980.41	70,415.5	63,221.07	56,379.01	49,872.11	43,683.98	37,799.04	32,202.48	26,880.21	21,818.82
forward+100bp	100,000	48,904.83	44,160.55	39,648.62	35,357.68	31,276.92	27,396.08	23,705.39	20,195.55	16,857.72	13,683.51
forward	100,000	35,460.82	32,020.75	28,749.16	25,637.8	22,678.85	19,864.86	17,188.74	14,643.76	12,223.51	9,921.89

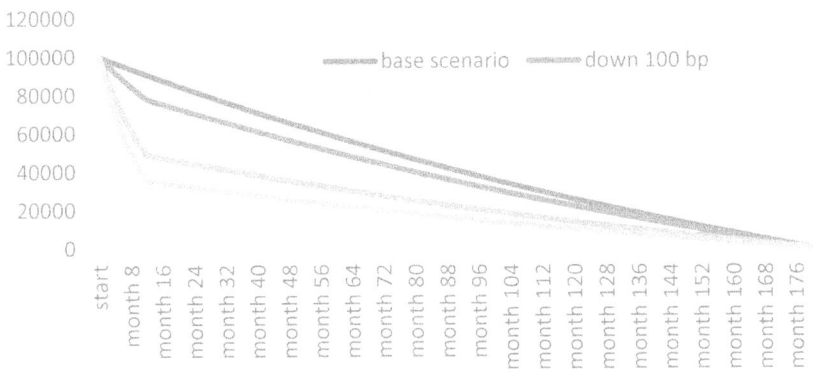

As well as the revenues from the pool:

Report Type	Annually					Scenario Comparison : Assets.loan book							
Scenario	Opening Balance	01/2016 - 12/2016	01/2017 - 12/2017	01/2018 - 12/2018	01/2019 - 12/2019	01/2020 - 12/2020	01/2021 - 12/2021	01/2022 - 12/2022	01/2023 - 12/2023	01/2024 - 12/2024	01/2025 - 12/2025	01/2026 - 12/2026	01/2027 - 12/2027	01/2028 - 12/2028
forward+300bp		4,785.95	4,333.62	3,903.43	3,494.32	3,105.24	2,735.22	2,383.33	2,048.65	1,730.44	1,427.75	1,139.95	866.27	605.99
forward+200bp		4,474.41	3,724.09	3,354.41	3,002.83	2,668.48	2,350.51	2,048.11	1,760.53	1,487.05	1,226.97	979.64	744.43	520.76
forward+100bp		3,680.46	2,335.53	2,103.69	1,883.21	1,673.52	1,474.1	1,284.46	1,104.11	932.59	769.48	614.37	466.86	326.59
forward		3,250.14	1,693.49	1,525.39	1,365.51	1,213.47	1,068.87	931.36	800.59	676.22	557.95	445.48	338.52	236.91

Notice that since the CPR is an annualized prepayment ratio and loans keep amortizing, the cumulative prepayment in percentage of the initial principal at the end of the wave of prepayments isn't equal to the CPR.

For the calibration of the pricing, we assume that the following prepayments were made in the year following the IR move, the other loans keeping their standard amortizing schedule.

scenario	CPR	Cumulative CPR after 1 year	Prepayments linked to shock
Current forward curve + 300 bp	5%	4.8%	0
Current forward curve + 200 bp	5% + 15% the first year	17.8%	13%
Current forward curve + 100 bp	5% + 60% the first year	47.7%	42.9%
Current forward curve	5% + 85% the first year	59.5%	55.7%

In our pricing, we will indeed assume these prepayments in percentage of the remaining principal when the shock is observed.

The prepayment curve will obviously have to be translated depending on the vintage of the loan. It is assumed that for vintages produced at higher market rate, the move of IR already triggered the wave of prepayment and the loan book stabilized. Indeed, in percentage of remaining loans, the percentage of loans which should never prepay increase in proportion:

Prepayments / loan	At the money	100 bp above money	150 bp above money
-100 bp	15%	45/85 = 53%	35/65 = 54%
-150 bp	20%	18%	8%
-200 bp	25%	6%	
-300 bp	20%		
Never exercise	15%	23%	38%

Pricing of the prepayment option for a linear amortizing loan, annual cost in bp

Duration of loans	10	15
At the money	19	32
100 bp above market	38	45
150 bp above market	51	55

The premium actually is also contingent on the non-exercise of the option: the customer pays it in its loan rate until it exercises.

Results are interesting:

- The current price of the option is not null despite the market conditions,
- The profitability of the loans made in the past is significantly affected by the increase in value of the prepayment option.
- This pricing was made assuming the percentage of customers who shall never exercise to be constant. This assumption may be wrong considering the media effect we observe currently.

We also tested for a same loan (at the money, duration 15 years) different prepayment curves to see the impact on the option value:

Prepayment curve	Option value (bp)
Linear increase up to 300 bp, 10% never prepaying	33
Slow prepayments below 100 bp then up to 300 bp	34
High prepayments below 100 bp getting down	31

The sensitivity to the slope of the curve is relatively negligible in comparison of the other assumptions. What matters is really the terminal point, here - 300 bp for 90% of the vintage being prepaid.

Conclusion

The banks too often do not value properly the prepayment option that they provide to their customers. As observed, moves can be massive with vintages of fixed rate loans being almost fully prepaid in case of a move of more than 300 bps.

The curve of prepayment as a function of interest rates is difficult to precisely assess but the value of the option is more impacted by an error on the market parameters than on the shape of the curve.

Monte-Carlo simulation methodology seems more accurate at describing the temporality of a wave of prepayments but its use for pricing the option raise the issue of the calibration of the parameters and of the calculation time.

Our approach has the advantage of representing the behavior of the subscribers in a pragmatic way. It is also pretty flexible and allows to perform various simulations, which is the only solution because of the lack of data, in order to model the customers' behavior.

More importantly, all the underlying calibration processes will lead naturally to a hedging strategy, which will be consistent with the modeling of the borrowers' behavior.

Prepayment options are complex to model, to price and to manage but their impact is massive on the balance sheet and incomes statement in case of significant decrease in IR. All the banks are currently facing the same challenging environment, a stress scenario of "Japanese crisis" with waves of prepayments.

References

"Bear Stearns Quick Guide to Agency MBS"

"Modeling the dynamics of Borrower Attributes", Bear Stearns FAST 2002.

"Short term prepayment Estimates" Bear Stearns FAST 2008.

"Modeling the financial management of a commercial bank" S. Moulin, ALM-Vision 2016.

"An empirical analysis of pricing of MBS", K.Dunn & K. Singleton, Journal of Finance, vol. 38, May 1983.

"Prepayment and the valuation of MBS", E. Swartz & W. Torous, Journal of Finance, vol. 44-2, June 1989

"Rational prepayments and the valuation of collateralized mortgage obligations", J. Mc Connell, Journal of Finance, vol. 49-3, July 1994

"Pricing and hedging prepayment risk", M. Sherries, actuarial review.

PRICING REAL ESTATE, an elegant modeling

Pricing real estate is nowadays considered rather an expert exercise without formal link with interest rates. However, with the developments of regulatory risk measurement, sensitivity of real estate investments to interest rates becomes adamant. This is not only useful from a risk perspective but also provides an interesting insight on the relative value of the market compared to other investments.

Indeed, real estate appears more and more as a beautiful long-term asset class, with good protection against inflation, good risk premium for a reasonable liquidity risk and a low valuation risk in time of market crisis.

Modeling shows in addition that the sensitivity of prices to IR is lower than anticipated with an asymmetrical behavior, making Real Estate an even better class of assets for the current environment (this obvious observation challenge the stress test defined in Solvency II standard model).

But most models use pure econometrical macro-economic methodologies, observing rather than explaining the prices movements. We try to rather explain pricing in order to integrate in a better way Real Estate in ALM modeling using three parameters, interest rates, inflation and a correlation link depending on intrinsic characteristics of each real estate market.

Real estate remains a fundamental class of assets but its stake in the global allocations of investors that we observe can vary widely with some long term institutional having very low exposures to R.E. whereas some family offices take much more significant positions.

Still, the market is illiquid and require deep expertise since each subclasses of Real Estate investments are different and react differently to modifications of the economic environment.

Pricing methodology used in the industry for commercial R.E.

Prices P(r) are made in reference with the yield y(r) of the investment, as a function of long-term interest rate r for 1 unit of net rent (that is after cost), price is then equal to:

$$P(r) = \frac{1}{y(r)} \text{ per unit of rent.}$$

The pricing is in obvious analogy with equities' "Price Earning Ratio". The yield is indeed the rent to price ratio that is the inverse of a "Price Rent Ratio".

Subsequently, the sensitivity of real estate to long-term interest rate r is simple:

$$\text{sensitivity} = -\frac{\partial \ln P(r)}{\partial r} = \frac{y'(r)}{y(r)} = P(r).y'(r)$$

This formula is generic since we have no information on the sensitivity of the yield to interest rates.

Link between return and access to leverage

Actually, professional investors use a leverage 1/(1-k), borrowing k.P(r) at interest rate r + spread (spread is currently around 200 bp, relatively stable these last years).

k is usually between 60% and 80% depending on the market. k wasn't really sensitive to interest rate even during the crisis but rather to the volatility of the price of real estate.

Investors indeed commit the capital (1-k).P(r) and their return on investment becomes, after costs of real estate management and without taking into account inflation:

$$ROE = \frac{y(r).P(r) - k.P(r).(r+spread)}{(1-k).P(r)}$$

$$ROE = \frac{1}{1-k}.\left[y(r) - k.(r+spread)\right]$$

$$y(r) = (1-k).ROE + k.(r+spread)$$

If we note *ROE=r+rp* where *rp* is the risk premium expected by investors over long term rate *r*, the expression becomes:

$$y(r) = r + (1-k).rp + k.spread$$

The yield in this model is logically equals to the interest rate plus the weighted average between the risk premium on the money invested and the cost of borrowing, reduced by the frictional costs of management.

So the derivative **if one assumes that neither k, spread and rp depend on interest rates**:

$$y'(r) = 1$$

And the sensitivity becomes:

$$sensitivity = P(r).y'(r) = P(r) = \frac{1}{y(r)}$$

What is interesting in this expression is that the formula doesn't need any other information than the yield.

The risk premium requested by investor comes from the previous relationship:

$$rp = \frac{1}{1-k}.\left[y - r - k.spread\right]$$

Obviously, as long-term investments, RE investments have a long duration, the longest currently observed on the market (equities for comparison have a duration equal to PER+1 that is currently around 11 years).

yield	5.5%	6.0%	6.5%
Price = 1/yield	18.18	16.67	15.38
Long-term rate r	1.10%	1.50%	1.90%
cost	20%	20%	20%
sensitivity	22.7	20.8	19.2
bank spread	2%	2%	2%
leverage k	80%	80%	80%
ROE	9.6%	10.0%	10.4%
risk premium	8.50%	8.50%	8.50%

The sensitivity seems extremely high, too high to express correctly the recent observations of the R.E. market. However, it provides a first view on the real approach of R.E. professional investors. Interviews with expert investors specialized in R.E. confirms that they look first at the yield and ROE after leverage and seek opportunities depending on the economic cycle. One of the main area of opportunities is that the market doesn't adjust to the moves of interest rates instantaneously and real estate market can become very attractive as it is the case today with a high risk premium, higher sometimes than for equity, for a risk often lower.

Pricing using a DDM methodology

Actually, the previous formula doesn't express the true expected return on a real estate investment. Return on RE investment can indeed be more attractive because rents are usually indexed on inflation. Let assume an investment made at time t_0 at a yield of y_0 and for a price P_0 for 1 unit of rent, with the relation: $P_0 = \dfrac{1}{y_0}$.

We note i_t the instantaneous rate of growth of inflation (whatever inflation indexation the contract refers to) at time t and $I_t = \int_{s=0}^{t} I_s . i_s . ds = e^{\int_0^t i(s) ds}$ the cumulated inflation at t.

A time t, this investment shall generate I_t (paid end of period) for an initial unit of rent and its price becomes $P_t = \dfrac{I_t}{y_t}$

$$P_t = \frac{I_t}{y_t} = \frac{I_t}{\left[i(t) + r_{real}(t) + (1-k).rp + k.spread\right]} \quad (1)$$

The formula translates the increase of price in time with inflation but doesn't give a satisfying view on the sensitivity, neither explains where the rule used by professionals for pricing (the inverse of the yield) comes from.

A classical modeling is to apply the Dividend Discount Model to Real Estate with an initial rent supposed to be equal to 1:

$$P_t = \sum_{s>t} \frac{I_{s-1}}{(1 + r_s(t) + \mu_t)^{s-t}}$$

For a constant anticipated inflation rate i_t (actually it is rather the anticipated construction cost index which was historically higher than inflation) and a flat IR curve r_t, formula becomes:

$$P_t = \frac{I_t}{1+i_t} \cdot \sum_{s>t} \left(\frac{1+i_t}{1+r_t+\mu_t}\right)^{s-t} = \frac{I_t}{1+r_t+\mu} \cdot \sum_{s\geq 0} \left(\frac{1+i_t}{1+r_t+\mu_t}\right)^{s} \quad (2)$$

$$P_t = \frac{I_t}{r_t + \mu_t - i_t} = \frac{I_t}{r_{real}(t) + \mu_t} = \frac{I_t}{y_t}$$

(formulas are identical in continuous models)

Indeed, professionals are using a simple DDM to price their investment.

The price formula (2) depends on the risk premium µ which expresses the global risk related to a RE investment. More interesting, the formula see the yield as related to the real interest rate instead of the absolute interest rate, plus the risk premium.

$$y_t = r_{real}(t) + \mu_t = r_t - i_t + \mu_t$$

This modeling explains why yields seem more stable than interest rates: if inflation remains stable, the yield shall move only with the real interest rate. However, as we have observed these last years, the real interest rate was impacted by the decrease of the absolute interest rate.

We keep the formula:

$$sensitivity = P(r).y'(r) = I_t . \frac{y'(r)}{y(r)} = -I_t . \frac{\partial \ln y(r)}{\partial r}$$

$$sensitivity = -I_t . \frac{\partial \ln\left[r_{real}(t) + \mu_t\right]}{\partial r} = -I_t . \frac{\partial \ln\left[r(t) - i_t + \mu_t\right]}{\partial r}$$

- Assuming μ and i independent of the interest rates, the sensitivity becomes:

$$sensitivity = \frac{I_t}{r_t + \mu - i_t} = \frac{I_t}{r_{real}(t) + \mu} = \frac{I_t}{y_t}$$

And the $duration = I_t . \frac{1 + r_t + \mu_t}{r_t - i_t + \mu_t} = I_t . \frac{1 + y_t + i_t}{y_t}$

- Assuming that inflation and absolute interest rates are linked with $r_t = i_t + r_{real}(t)$ and r_{real} is independent of the absolute interest rates, the sensitivity becomes 0 ! Yields should move only with the real interest rates.

- The real model seems to be between these two extreme schemes. Indeed, these last years, we have observed strange relationships between IR and real IR with the inflation swap markets pricing negative real interest rates following the quantitative easing and the pressures on govies' yields due to the purchases made by the ECB. Forward inflation rates implied by the market were also sometimes difficult to explain because of these liquidity issues. Let write in a more generic way that:

$$i_t = \beta_t . r_t + \varepsilon_t$$

$$sensitivity = -I_t . \frac{\partial \ln\left[r_t . (1 - \beta_t) - \varepsilon_t\right]}{\partial r} = (1 - \beta_t) . \frac{I_t}{y_t}$$

$$duration = (1 - \beta_t) . I_t . \frac{1 + y_t + i_t}{y_t}$$

The parameter $β_t$ depends on the state of the economy. It is the classical "beta" of an economic variable, the indexation, to interest rate. For ALM modeling, it makes sense to link this indexation with inflation in order to reduce the number of parameters and attend to capture the links between R.E. prices and the other parameters describing the state of the economy.

The originality of the modeling is that we consider the indexation as linked to interest rates and not the opposite. This avoids problems with limits and allow modeling different type of indexation under scenario only referring to interest rates without getting into the debate of relationship between inflation CPI and interest rates. $β_t$ is supposed to be between 0 and 1 but this isn't mandatory since the other parameter may include a negative constant for example and an index can react more than the CPI to an increase of inflation.

The beta seems to increase when inflation increase or in period of economic uncertainty.

The realty is clearly better represented and explained by this third model but one element remain: beta seems depending on the class of Real Estate.

- Commercial R.E. yields are indexed for example in France on ICC (French building construction index price), which is decorrelated from CPI but correlated with interest rates. Indeed commercial R.E. beta is high and yield shows a lower correlation with interest rates than other classes. The result may also come from the fact that the commercial market is a pure professional market with a strong influence from leverage so IR. The result is a stable class of assets.
- Retail R.E. appears more sensitive to IR. At least for the relatively small movements observed these last two decades. Indeed, the estimated beta is low. The indexation with inflation is real but indirect (there is no contractual indexation of rent for example). It is because inflation and revenues are linked and real estate being the first budget of household, rent and prices mechanically adjust with their purchasing power, especially in a market without major unbalance between bid and offer of housing. However, many other elements have to be taken into account to explain the building of prices (see below).

Subsequently, IR seems to have a higher influence on prices than for commercial real estate.
- Specialized R.E. subclasses like health housing are relatively correlated with classical commercial Real Estate but with a higher beta translating the fact that this class of asset is structurally more stable.

The analysis we performed on these different markets show that the modeling using the beta methodology is the correct one. Still the estimation of beta remain the complex part of the work and presents some asymmetry.

Statistical observation

On long term, analysis of data for the French market gives:

- ✓ Estimated beta of 0.7 between interest rates and ICC (the construction index used for indexation) but with weak statistical correlation as it is obvious in the two graphs below

IR and ICC historical datas

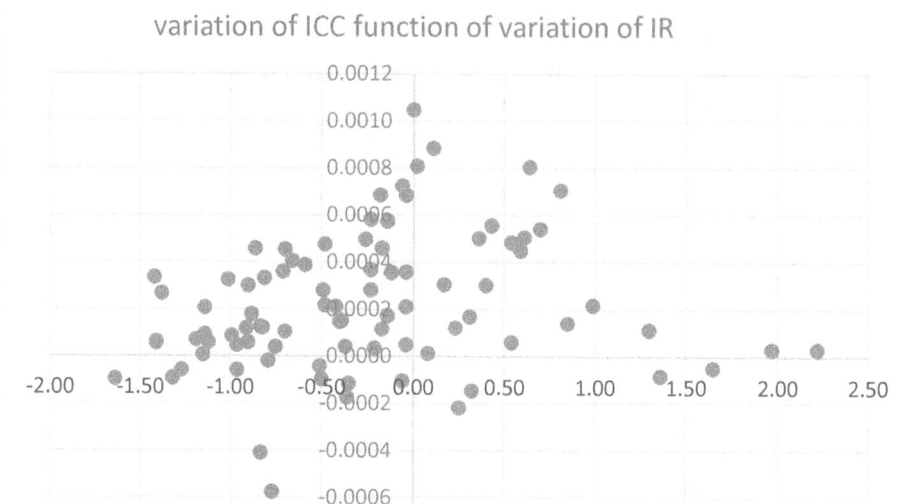

- ✓ a beta of 0.25 between CPI and IR. Here again, the estimations aren't strong with weak statistical tests[9].

---

[9] This obviously challenges the efficiency of the micro-management of inflation by central bank through interest rates. It seems that inflation is a very complex phenomena and influence through interest rates management is a long-term macro-effect. Effect appears more direct on growth (growth is then supposed to generate inflation).

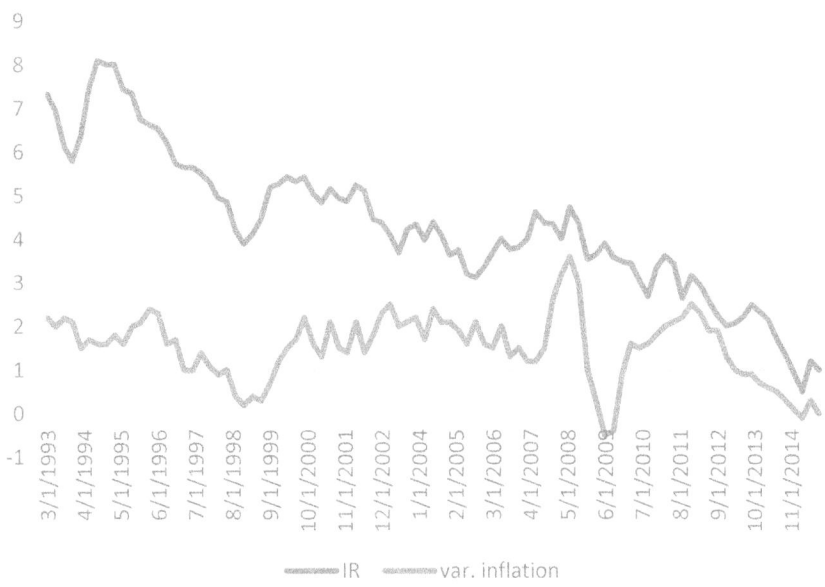

The impact is obviously significant on the sensitivity of Real Estate to IR:

Commercial Real Estate				Housing Real Estate			
yield	5.50%	5.80%	6.10%	yield	5.50%	6.25%	7.00%
Price = 1/yield	18.18	17.24	16.39	Price = 1/yield	18.18	16.00	14.29
long term rate r	1.00%	2.00%	3.00%	long term rate r	1.00%	2.00%	3.00%
indexation	1.00%	1.70%	2.40%	indexation	1.00%	1.25%	1.50%
costs	20%	20%	20%	costs	20%	20%	20%
beta	70%	70%	70%	beta	25%	25%	25%
sensitivity	**6.8**	**6.5**	**6.1**	**sensitivity**	**17.0**	**15.0**	**13.4**
duration	7.3	7.0	6.7	duration	18.2	16.1	14.5
spread bank	2%	2%	2%	spread bank	2%	2%	2%
leverage k	80%	80%	80%	leverage k	80%	80%	80%
ROE	10.0%	7.2%	4.4%	ROE	10.0%	9.0%	8.0%
risk premium	5.50%	5.50%	5.50%	risk premium	5.50%	5.50%	5.50%

An explanation to the difference of beta between asset classes is due to the fact that indexation is of different nature with the asset class:

- ✓ in commercial R.E., indexation is to the construction index which is linked to IR (it wasn't correlated strongly to inflation these last years) and beta appears to be rather around 0.7.
- ✓ in retail R.E., indexation is indirect through the mechanism of pricing by household of their housing budget and beta was lower around 0.25. Interest rates have had a stronger effect on prices these last years.

The model is slightly modified since there is some degrees of independence between inflation parameter and Real Estate indexation, this degree of independence depends on the R.E. market.

Pricing mechanism for retail housing

In most markets, housing is households' first budget with 25% to 40% of their spending dedicated to housing. Inside this budget, households try to use as much leverage as possibly available through the banking system which provides them with a purchasing power: the longer they can borrow, the lower the interest rates, the higher their budget. Market prices then adjust to balance offer and demand per area (the famous American MSA).

In period of recession, two conflicting phenomena are observed: interest rates are getting down pushing prices up but households' budget and more importantly expected future budgets are also getting down whereas in parallel, risk increasing, banks are widening their spread and tightening their lending criteria. Indexation is indeed reduced compared to interest rates: beta is higher than estimated using the correlation between CPI and interest rates.

Risk premium in DDM

Using both formula (1) and (2), we get the logical relation with the spread requested by the bank for the senior tranche and the risk premium requested by investors for the equity tranche:

$$\mu = (1-k).rp + k.spread$$

The total risk is the weighted average of the risks priced for the first tranche (the equity tranche purchased by customers) and the senior tranche (purchased by the bank).

Actually, the leverage k and the risk premium *rp* are also parameters depending on other elements: *rp*, *spread*, market volatility and… the copula correlations between tranches.

The dividend discount model doesn't give indeed much more indication, just helping expressing the link between the different risk premiums.

Time effect in Real Estate and stress scenarios

Stress testing

We observe very few examples of R.E. market crashing quickly. Evolutions are usually progressive with a lag between 6 months and 3 years. Even the 2008 US crash didn't take place in one night but it took 4 years to the Home Price Index (HPI) to lose 19%.

Still certain specific area and sectors observed faster and more violent moves with prices down 50% in one year.

The S&P/Case-Shiller index which focus on single family houses in 10 metropolitan areas lost 27% in the same period of 4 years.

During this period, a R.E. portfolio still may generate revenues. With yield significantly above refunding rates, real estate investments appear indeed attractive:

- solid cash flow visibility
- relatively stable prices out of bubble effects
- slow variation of prices
- protection against inflation
- leverage available and significant spread in many markets

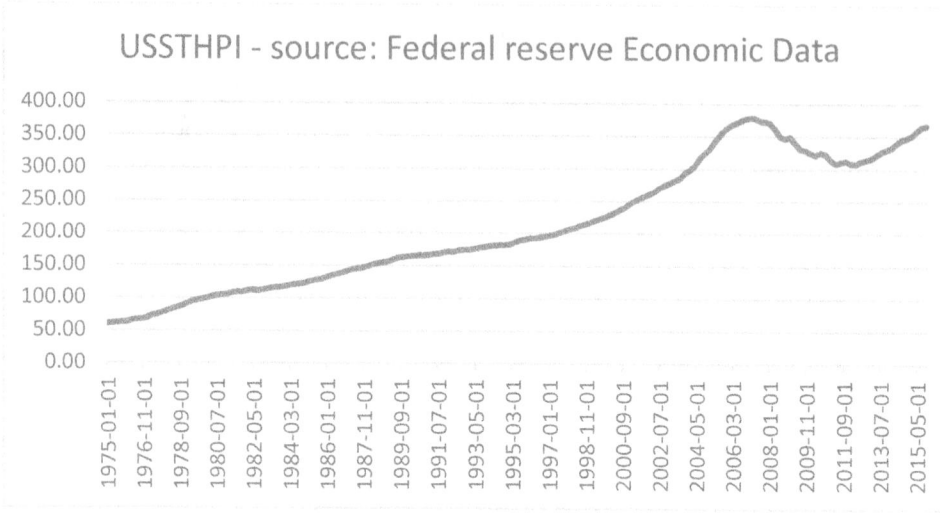

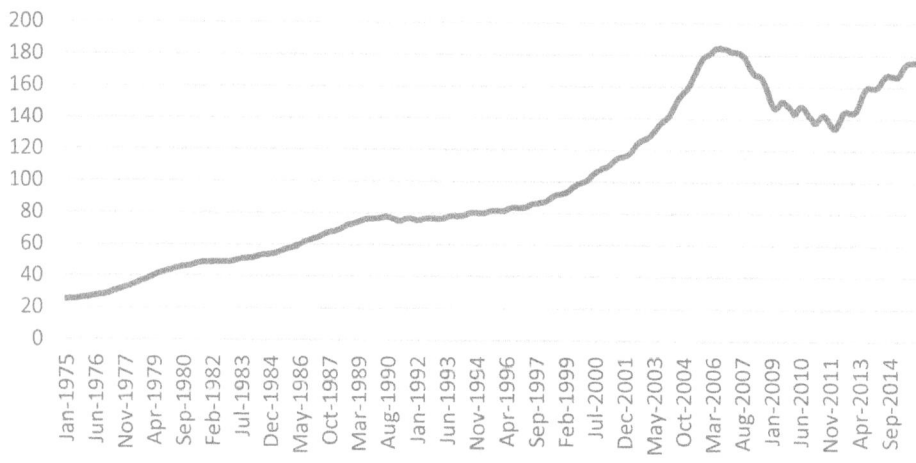

All these elements justify getting away from standard stress testing methodology for adopting more precise models. This is especially true for insurance companies. Under Solvency II standard methodology, one must assume a 25% loss stress test at the horizon of 1 year (with a probability of occurrence of 1 time every 200 years). This assumption appears very harsh compared to what was observed in the past. It is in addition used with significant correlation with equity: 75% and spread: 50%.

If we can accept the idea that a bubble can occur at least one time every 200 years or that an exceptional event can every 200 years generate a collapse of the R.E. market, this modeling isn't taking into account the specificities of each present situation. Bubbles are obviously unpredictable, still statistical datas give signals which if they are used regularly can result in a more realistic modeling (the first one indicator being the past growth of prices in the last 5/2/1 years compared to inflation).

As an example, in an environment characterized, as it is today the case in Europe by low growth, low inflation, no demographic pressure, the probability of seeing a violent surge of inflation is null, a shock to real estate can't come from such a scenario. Identically, banks didn't lose their criteria of loans' acceptance. Evolutions in the behavior of the population are also very progressive, as well for consumption (with internet shopping competing against street shopping) than for work (with the development of internet working). A scenario of real estate crash should come only from geo-strategical events: civil war, external attack, pandemic, collapse of the state because of an excessive debt... Out of these extreme events, a stressed economic scenario on a well diversified portfolio of real estate would rather result in a devaluation around 10/15%, which is already massive. But with real estate yields around 3 to 6%, it means a loss of wealth for investors below 10%, a very reasonable risk.

Optimum refunding of R.E. investments

The choice between a refunding at fixed rate or at variable rate depends on several parameters:

-the banks' offer of course but currently most banks offer both types of rates even though they sometimes encourage customers to choose fixed rate,

- the probability of renegotiating or prepaying the loan. This is a key point and not only in case of scheduled resale. Indeed, the spread charged by banks depends on risk, mostly the LTV and the soundness of the tenant. With time, LTV decreases. So does the risk for the bank and subsequently, the spread can be significantly reduced in case of renegotiation.

- the sensitivity of rent to inflation. As we have seen however, there is a lag between the IR move and the variation of the indexation. IR react real time and in anticipation whereas indices react slower.

The beta gives the sensitivity of the interest rates to the inflation indexation of the rent. Formally, an investor can borrow at variable rate up to *beta/k* with a natural statistical hedge from the indexation of its rent during the life of the loan. Actually, because of the lag between interest rate and indexation move, a better IR indexation to negotiate with banks would be for example an average of the E3M rate over the last 6 months. This allows smoothing the day-to-day moves of short-term rate.

A second element to take into account is the global economic balance of the deal: IR random movement out of any significant variation of anticipated inflation can be significant. An investor able to accept the hazard relating to these moves has interest to borrow a bit more at variable rate. A less flexible investor should reduce the part of loan at variable rate.

Finally, beta can change with what we called a change of economic regime. There is indeed a level of uncertainty in the estimation of the parameter in case for example of a surge of inflation: renters challenging the indexation, government steeping in... It is therefore cautious to buy systematically some out of the money cap to hedge this tail risk on the variable rate loan. In the same way, short-term interest rates are more volatile than long-term rates and can vary significantly from their theoretical value, as it was the case at the beginning of the 90s.

Globally, it appears that investors have too much the tendency to borrow fixed rate without paying enough attention to the prepayment clauses and the sensitivity of their rents to inflation. This is a general observation even though each situation requires a specific analysis and pricing: the price of these options, caps or prepayment options, depend on the volatility of the market and the spread between variable rate and fixed rate loan varies.

Other elements to take into account in R.E. pricing

As we have seen, the yields priced by the market are impacted by many parameters, which are translated in the choice of beta. We gathered some data on the three last years. It confirms the yields aren't following the long term interest rate with strong sensitivity (whereas the inflation effect was small these last years).

Prices have some level of independence between the major Real Estate classes of assets: retail, offices, commercial real estate and specialized RE (health care, warehousing, social sector…) because of their various sensitivity to the different macro-economic parameters:

- Interest rates: naturally, as predicted by the DDM, when IR go down, prices have a tendency to get up. However, the formula isn't as predictable due to the limited access to credit and the correlation between IR decrease and economic downturn. In an environment where there is a shortage of housing, decrease of interest rates push faster prices up since prices adjust in order to maintain the same allocation of revenues dedicated to housing in the budget of buyers.

- Equity markets: some studies show direct correlation between both markets equities and real estate whereas other show a strong resilience of real estate to a bad stock market. The dependence seems indeed function of the culture of the country and characteristics of the real estate market (taxes, banks' flexibility, culture of renovation for resale, culture of stock exchange investments, profile of the companies listed on the stock exchange…). At the beginning of the 2000's years, the equity market collapsed in the USA but the housing market remained bullish.

- Economic growth and political stability have a direct impact on housing prices. Indeed prices are obviously under pressure to decrease in difficult times. Real estate is still the first asset in the wealth of household and mortgages are their first liability.

Economic cycles have therefore a direct impact on real estate prices and transactions as well as on consumption. Commercial real estate shows a similar pattern for more direct reasons (impact of the economic situation to the need of premises of corporations). The most cyclical subclass of real estate is indeed obviously the office building area and **offices real estate subclass is often seen as a direct exposure first to the growth of a country. Similarly, commercial real estate is first an exposure to the consumption** (out of the major trend implied by internet). And inversely, retail housing prices are a key element for defining the household consumption growth. Long term trends between real estate and growth are unchallengeable with solid gains in real estate markets during the period of economic growth of the 80s and the 2000s and period of lower price appreciation or decline during the period of economic slowdown or recession of the 90s and since 2008.

- Balance between offer and demand of housing. In a market where there is an insufficient offer of housing, prices are pushed structurally up. Household have a tendency to increase their budget allocated to housing until they reach a ceiling above which the offer of loans disappear: The rule of maximum 1/3 of revenues dedicated to housing loans seems to be relatively stable. Household try then to adapt to increasing prices generated by a shortage of offer by reducing the size of their dwelling until they are forced to move to cheaper area. In this configuration, sensitivity to IR increases.

- Offer by banks: if banks expand duration of loans, this push prices up, especially in case of shortage of offer. The previous rule actually applies and the more easy the access to credit, the higher the probability to see an artificial increase in prices. This phenomena can even result in the **creation of bubbles** as in Ireland or in the USA[10]. The possibility for the banks to easily refund their

---

[10] It is interesting to notice that many studies in 2005-2007 successfully linked the increases of housing prices in the USA, Ireland, UK and Australia to the easing of borrowings constraints

balance sheet on the international market is identically facilitating the increase of R.E. prices up to the creation of bubbles and there are evidences of correlation between the current account deficit of a country and its R.E. prices driving up.

- Lag effect: adjustments in prices to a new environment isn't immediate and real estate often react progressively with 6 months of lag. This is due to the fact that there are several months between the decision of investment/disinvestment and its implementation. R.E. is indeed more sensitive to the average moves than instantaneous moves which enhance the stability of the asset class (but also makes its recovery in case of collapse of the market much slower).

- Studies show that about 30% of housing prices moves are directly linked to the world growth: indeed, R.E. is no longer a pure local market and **modeling must be integrated in global worldwide allocations**, with the first bet taken on global growth. This fact is reinforced by the importance of R.E. market on growth: counting for about 20% of GDP, housing market has a direct impact too on the global activity as was experienced in the USA in 2008.

The **estimation of Beta is the result of a full classical scoring methodology**. Its main difficulty remains on identifying the right parameters.

Conclusion

All these short term and long term elements driving R.E. prices translate in the coefficient beta defining the link between interest rates and the implicit or explicit indexation of real estate. The methodology we propose is the simplest one since it use for modeling a constant beta. The determination of this parameter shall be made on a case by case basis. For stress testing, one must modify the parameter assuming a change of configuration of the Real Estate market as it happened during

---

without drawing the final conclusion on the unsustainability of the move. Australia and UK may indeed just be the next bubbles waiting to burst.

the creation of the R.E. bubble in Spain, USA and Ireland between 2003 and 2008.

If the three key parameters explaining R.E. markets moves are the interest rates, the equity market (which is the weakest) and the growth national product (which is the strongest in long term), independently from the changes of characteristics of the market (behavior of households and lenders, taxes incitation, population growth...), the translation of their evolution in R.E. prices are very progressive and the lag can be between 6 months and three years. This can be translated in simulations by defining a vector of beta.

Real Estate is a fundamental class of assets in a strategic allocation. It is crucial to consider carefully its modeling and to document, as always, the calculation of the beta parameter. For investors, getting more precise provide a much more realistic view on potential stress tests.

References

✓ *House prices, interest rates and macroeconomic fluctuations: international evidence* by C. Otrok and M. E. Terrones, feb. 2005, IMF

✓ *Explaining changes in house prices,* BIS quarterly review part. 6, September 2002, by G. Sutton

✓ *House price booms, current account deficits and low interest rates,* Federal reserve bank of New York staff reports, A. Ferrero, jan. 2012

✓ *House prices, interest rates and the mortgage market meltdown,* Columbia Business School, by C. Mayer and R. Hubbard,

✓ *The baby boom: predictability in house prices and interest rates,* nov. 2005 by R. Martin

✓ *The rise and fall of the first global real estate bubble,* by G. Bernardos, Paradigmes, june 2009

✓ *The sources of house price change: identifying liquidity shocks to the housing market,* by P. de La Paz and M. White, 2013

✓ *What drives housing price dynamics: cross-country evidence* by K. Tsatsaronis and H. Zhu, BIS

The NEW STANDARD for INTEREST RATE RISK in the BANKING BOOK defined by the BASEL COMMITTEE on Banking Supervision: Finally, ALM makes its revolution.

Summary

The Basel Committee released in April 2016 its new directive d368 *Interest Rate Risk in the Banking Book* ("IRRBB"). This directive finally replaces the former text of July 2004[11] which was no more adapted from a methodological point of view but which was rich in recommendations and already included the fundamental principles to follow for managing interest rate risk[12] in the banking book. Indeed, the new text does not appear as a break away from but rather as a continuation on an area that was neglected during the crisis. Where the text is revolutionary is that the regulator moved significantly away from a position of general but often vague principles to a much more demanding quality of management and modeling of IRRBB.

Indeed, <u>this text appears fundamental and raises the bar at the highest technical level</u>, requiring banks to improve their methodologies, their expertise and to review their setup in a very short period of time.

It also reassesses the responsibility of the management, a repeating leitmotiv since the crisis which should lead inevitably to the granting of

---

[11] BCBS 108, July 2004, "Principles for the management and supervision of interest rate risk"
[12] The text inspired both the creation of ALM-Solutions® software and a significant part of Serge Moulin's book *"Modélisation de la gestion financière d'une banque commerciale"*, 2012, forthcoming 2016 english translation *"Modeling the financial management of a commercial bank"*.

licensing for executive officers of banks in the EU (and their removal in case of resolution).

The text is complex, dense and still includes some grey areas. It is based on the latest improvements made in ALM, it requires to value almost "marked to model" the full balance sheet and it definitely deserves comments.

For ALM-VISION, it is the translation into the regulation of most of the concepts that we introduced five years ago.

Presentation of the new regulation

A dual approach starting December 31st 2017

The first calculation on the new standard will have to be produced with the figures of December 31st 2017.

It shall apply to all internationally active banks and very likely, national regulators will require the same methodology to be adopted by smaller institutions.

The IRRBB risk is divided into three components:

1. Gap risk which describe the impact of mismatch in term of IR duration of assets and liabilities.
2. Basis risk which describes the risk of mismatch between IR indexes.
3. Options risk which can be automatic and behavioral.

To these three risks is added the credit spread risk in the banking book (CSRBB) between assets and liabilities (this last risk actually killed Dexia): the CSRBB component is a new fundamental addition to the regulation.

The regulator finally acknowledges that two measures of risks must be made:

1. The so called "economic value" variation measure: this "static balance sheet" methodology is privileged by regulators since it avoids having to make assumptions on future production (volumes and margin) and corresponds to its concern, which is

having to step in, take over the management of an institution and put it in run off.
2. The earnings-based measures, which is used by institutions as this is the only way to answer the key question: what is the impact on my earnings of the following economic scenario?

It is interesting to note that for the first time, the <u>regulator acknowledges that the static economic value methodology "could run the risk of earnings volatility"</u>. This is a great progress for a methodology which has serious fundamental limitations (see below) but was still recently considered as unchallengeable. The chosen dual approach seems indeed extremely reasonable:

- The first calculation appears as a conventional ratio to respect, its goal being to translate as accurately as possible a variation of economic value of a balance sheet, the equivalent of the "Value In Force" insurance notion, should the bank stop its activities, be put in run off under certain assumptions.
- The second calculation provides the real sensitivity of the incomes statement to an economic scenario.

The text is made of two parts: a definition and methodology of calculation of IRRBB risk and a set of operational requirements, the principles, in term of organization of ALM.

9 key principles for banks

Principle 1: IRRBB is an important risk for all banks that must be specifically identified, measured, monitored and controlled. In addition, banks should monitor and assess CSRBB.

If this principle appears as common sense, it is <u>the first time that the regulation requires a real global approach in term of modeling of the balance sheet, one that is thorough and consistent</u>.

The regulator also emphasizes the fact that since modeling a balance sheet is a heavy task, this should be made also for "business planning and budgeting activities". This is very important in order to get a rational and homogeneous approach of the financial management of the balance sheet: a good modeling allows to produce and modify budgets quickly, to plan its strategy over the next years, to understand its liquidity risk and its IRRBB.

The text integrates the IRRBB into the complete chain of processes of the bank and requires it to perform a full ALM analysis before entering into a new product or activity.

Finally, commercial margin and spread risk (CSRBB) must be monitored (that is building historical data and analyzing it).

Principle 2: the governing body of each bank is responsible for oversight of the IRRBB management framework... Banks must have an adequate IRRBB management framework, involving regular independent reviews and evaluations of the effectiveness of the system.

This second principle is in the continuation of the Basel III strategy of making the board and top management accountable. This obvious and positive reaction to the abuses of the financial crisis where no management was really threatened for wrong-doing is yet to be fully implemented. If some regulators begin to refuse accrediting as fit and proper for top positions some candidates, who, despite their obvious political qualities, are clearly not experienced or technically equipped to assume their responsibilities, the broad majority of regulators still simply register the decisions of the banks. It is our opinion that this principle shall be translated into formal licenses with formal check on expertise and experience. And with the automatic and systematic removal of the license in case of involvement in a serious issue[13].

---

[13] We are aware of two recent examples of this toughening of the behavior of regulators: one in Europe refused to accredit someone obviously not technically qualified as fit and proper for the position of CRO. The other example is in Russia where the central bank, after taking over a financial institution during the recent crisis, removed all the licenses of the top management without entering into the exercise of asserting each individual involvement in the collapse of the entity. We consider this firmness as the only way for the regulators of having efficient whistleblowing and accountable management.

The second significant evolution of the regulation is that it now requires regular independent reviews and evaluations of the effectiveness of the system: the regulator leaves the banks to choose if this must be made by the internal control or a specialized external entity (§27). It is our opinion that the matter is so technical that only specialized independent external firms could provide board and top management with an effective independent review[14] and that it would be wise for the institution to benchmark and challenge their teams on a regular basis or in case of significant change.

The regulator insists again (as in the previous text) to get "comprehensive IRRBB reporting and review", that is "no black box".

The rest of the principle expands to the IRRBB, the good practices of documentation, defined limits, segregation of duties, independence between the actors involved and adequate systems and control...

It requires a (at least) <u>semiannual information to the board</u> on the IRRBB exposure with complete and comprehensive documentation. It also <u>requires some members of the board to be fit and proper</u> to understand this information and to engage into a dialogue with the specialists involved (which means that some boards will have to be trained or reinforced).

Principle 3: The bank's risk appetite for IRRBB should be articulated in terms of the risk to both economic value and earnings...

<u>Policy limits must be applied on a consolidated basis and individually or per book depending on the complexity of the activity.</u>

Limits must be enforced. Situations that are over the limit must be escalated.

The hedging strategy must be modeled MtM, formally analyzed and validated: this point is made in order to avoid a Dexia-like situation where

---

[14] We have been involved in several emergency reviews recently where internal audit did not raise the fundamental issue, just focusing on the formalizing of the ALM policy because they did not have the adequate experience, expertise and independence.

the hedging book itself becomes part of the issue, one of the major dangers of micro-hedging (including margin call financing).

Stress scenarios used to define limits must take into account historical data, observed volatility and time required by the management to mitigate exposure: this requirement means that institutions must have a real scientific approach to the generation of their stress scenarios. It is in the spirit of the Basel III recommendation to consider any type of possible scenario, "even the most unlikely".

Principle 4: measurement of IRRBB should be based on outcomes of both economic value and earnings-based measures, arising from a wide and appropriate range of IR shock and stress scenario.

The regulator put officially the two methodologies, equity economic value variation and earnings variation, at the same level as "complementary"[15].

If variation of the economic value of equity does give an indication of the change in value of the balance sheet under certain assumptions of sensitivity for no maturity assets, it however does not capture the real sensitivity of the value of the bank to IR shocks since new production is not taken into account.

Inversely, earnings sensitivity is more accurately estimated short-term but as it is done in ALM-Solutions, serious modeling must always be longer term[16] even though accuracy decreases in time. It allows indeed to capture through a dividend discount model the global impact of the economic scenario on the value of the bank. This point is developed below since it is key to understanding the limits of the new rule on such a complex subject.

However, since the regulator requires both approaches and gives the possibility to the local regulator to expand the duration of the earnings

---

[15] We disagree with §34 under which economic value variation would price the change in value of the balance sheet whereas earnings analysis should be only short-term. Earnings analysis in our view should be longer term as the text mentions in the next lines.

[16] We usually recommend about 5 years with a minimum of 3 years, figures that figure also in the text.

simulation (the average duration of a balance sheet is around 5 years), there is no obvious loophole in the regulation[17] anymore.

The last interesting point to notice in this principle is that the regulator uses officially for the first time the concept of roll -"assume rollover"-, a notion that ALM-solutions was one of the first to introduce in Europe at a time where both regulators and most professionals refused to try to model the incomes statement globally: this is a fundamental improvement after years of useless debates about NIM (Net Interest Margin) modeling.

The regulator also clarifies in this fourth principle the fundamental difference between the two approaches:

- The economic value measures must provide an estimate of the instantaneous variation of value of the book of the bank (both assets and liabilities) in case it has to be liquidated. Strangely, the regulator did not push the logic further by simply considering NMD (No Maturity Deposit) as cash (that would very likely be the reality).
- The earning variation is the indicator useful for management to appreciate its exposure to IR on a going concern basis.

Both risks are normally opposite! (c.f. below). Notice that the regulator provides an explicit warning on the strategy of only hedging the economic value: "the Committee acknowledges the importance of managing IRRBB through both economic value and earnings-based measures. If a bank solely minimizes its economic value risk by matching the repricing of its assets with liabilities beyond the short term, it could run the risk of earnings volatility". So <u>the correct strategy is to minimize the variation of NIM the first years under the constraint of respecting the maximum EVE variation on stock allowed by the regulator.</u>

<u>Principle 4 requires to have a system in place that allows to run both analyses on multiple scenarios, not only on the 6 prescribed IR shocks.</u> As we mentioned previously, defining a scenario becomes a complete exercise

---

[17] Reminder that "static view + roll including of no maturity items roll = dynamic view", c.f. *"Modeling the financial management of a commercial bank"*, forthcoming 2016, chapter "static or dynamic gaps"

in ALM and regulation is requiring to get a formal process in place or to follow one provided by a specialized entity.

More surprisingly, "banks should assess the possible interaction of IRRBB with its related risks, as well as other risks (eg credit risk, liquidity risk)" (page 9. 41): <u>modeling needs to be global and scenario must integrate cross effects</u>: IR down, spread and LGD up for example or inflation up, LGD and spread stable, IR up and currency down…

Indeed, <u>modeling must also integrate spread risks</u>.

Finally, the regulator requires qualitative and quantitative reverse stress testing and back testing of its modeling.

Principle 5: in measuring IRRBB, key behavioral and modeling assumptions should be fully understood, conceptually sound and documented. Such assumptions should be rigorously tested and aligned with the bank's business strategies.

This principle first reassesses the former request by the regulator of "no black box". But it is much more demanding in term of methodology:

- prepayment modeling must be rigorous, both on loans and deposits with estimates to be done per scenario and exogenous variables to be integrated as much as possible.
- No Maturity Deposits "NMD" must also be analyzed accurately including in term of liquidity per scenario.
- <u>Analysis must be made per currency as well as globally, integrating the correlation between IR, FX and other variables</u>: this is a major change.
- Cap, floor, swaptions and other automatic options must be integrated in an exact way (many banks were still using pseudo-matrix of delta).

Assumptions and models must be constantly reviewed and challenged.

Principle 6: measurement systems and models used for IRRBB should be based on accurate data, and subject to appropriate documentation, testing and controls to give assurance on the accuracy of calculations...

This principle mentions implicitly that <u>perfect accounting reconciliation is not required</u>. This is important since it is useless and extremely expensive and time consuming. Indeed, the text makes it clear that input must be "accurate", automated as much as possible (the regulator implicitly acknowledges that some treatment will have to remain manual) and should capture "the major sources of IRRBB exposure". "The Management Information System should capture IR risk data on all the bank's *material* IRRBB exposures". The regulator validates that the goal is not to get reconciled at one euro with the books and records (an argument of the vendors of massive system to justify their high prices) but to have a good estimate of the major risks.

What is interesting is that <u>the regulation really focuses on the modeling rather than on the tool</u>. This was a leitmotiv in our vision of ALM: the most important asset is the ALM manager, his work, his capacity in analyzing and modeling. The system remains only a tool, designed to help him to think more freely, to focus on what is adding value: the models themselves. In the text, the regulator makes it very clear that it is only concerned by the modeling and results, not the system (which needs to work!).

Logically, a <u>system must be flexible enough to allow for quick changes in assumption: this implicitly means that banks must get an adapted system</u>. The system must allow for static as well as dynamic analysis and must be capable of adapting to new regulatory requirements[18].

The regulator adds a recommendation (point 53): "banks should not rely on a single measure of risk, given that risk management systems [notice the plural] tend to vary...". <u>This implies the requirement to have different methodologies of risk quantification but also implicitly, it implies to get at least a separate system for the ALM team and the ALM risk control team</u>

---

[18] To our dear customers accusing us of having sponsored the new regulation, we deny firmly this assertion even though we acknowledge that we could not have done better... :-)

(even though both use the same data). Having the same system for both teams increases the risk of missing a component of the IRRBB even though it ultimately simplifies the work of the Risk Control Team.

In terms of the governance process of the models, <u>the regulator requires the same quality than for other risk measurement processes making of ALM a full position in the bank with the classical triptych: financial management manages ALM, risk department measures and control the limits, and internal audit reviews that the process is respected. Executive management supervises and validates by delegation of the board, and in the end the board is the final decision maker.</u>

Notice that "IRRBB models might include those developed by third-party vendors". This is the first text where the role of the external expert is mentioned so fundamentally.

Principle 7: Measurement outcomes of IRRBB and hedging strategies should be reported to the governing body or to its delegates on a regular basis, at relevant levels of aggregation

This principle is the translation of one of the Basel committee's key finding following the crisis: boards and executive management must be accountable. They must meet their responsibilities and can't find excuse for not being informed of their risks. This very positive and good commune sense approach is now a repeated leitmotiv of regulators since the crisis. It should lead inevitably to the granting of licensing for executive officers of banks in the EU (and their removal in case of resolution). It is our opinion that these licenses or registrations should be expanded to some key risk functions, ALM risk supervisor being one of them.

Principle 8: information on the level of IRRBB exposure and practices for measuring and controlling IRRBB must be disclosed to the public on a regular basis.

This principle is the logical extension of the previous one and a way for the regulator to hold boards and executive management accountable: in case of a problem, a lawsuit from shareholders becomes very likely.

Banks shall disclose both ΔEVE and 12-months ΔNII with high accuracy both in term of quantitative figures (table B, see p.17 of d368) and methodology (table A, see p.16 of d368).

Principle 9: Capital adequacy for IRRBB must be specifically considered as part of the ICAAP

"Banks are responsible for evaluating the level of capital that they should hold": <u>the responsibility is on the board and executive management first, not the regulator</u>. For that, they should not rely only on supervisory assessments (point 73): this is a key point since some banks have a tendency to just calculate ratios because they have to, without actually understanding the function of these ratios. On the contrary, banks should perform a full exercise of appreciating the adequate level of risk and capital they consider adapted to their business[19].

3 principles for supervisors

- Principle 10: supervisors must monitor the overall exposure of the market and compare banks.
- Principle 11: regulators should review on a regular basis IRRBB and for that, they should employ specialist resources.
- Principle 12: supervisors must publish their criteria for identifying outlier banks... When a review reveals inadequate management or excessive risk, supervisors must require mitigation actions and/or additional capital.

The standardized framework

The framework is not mandatory and banks can do better! This is just a minimum in term of methodology.

Two calculations must be performed.

---

[19] Notice point 74, the typo "IRBBB"... The Basel Committee itself starts to get lost into its numerous acronyms!

Variation of the Economic Value of Equity: ΔEVE

The methodology remains based on the previous static gap approach.

- Automatic embedded options are ignored for the estimation of gaps.
- Common Equity Tier 1, fixed assets, intangible assets and equity exposures are considered as perpetual, never amortizing.
- All other assets and liabilities or equivalent off-balance sheet assets are split between 19 time buckets depending on their amortizing or repricing date.
- Coupons and spreads above variable rates have to be included (point 102) but rather (point 103) banks can choose to exclude spreads and deduct commercial margin on fixed rates loans.
- No Maturity Deposits "NMD" are split between retail transactional, retail non-transactional and wholesale. The conventional amortizing profile is free with limits in term of overnight and average duration (cap at 5, 4.5 and 4 years).
- CPR must be included with a cap at 100%. They shall vary per scenario. Interest and notional CF must take into account prepayments. They apply to both assets and liabilities (term deposits).

<u>EVE is calculated per scenario and per currency representing more than 5% of the banking book</u> assets or liabilities as follow:

- The discount factor is exponential[20]. The rate is not defined and can include a spread, but this shall have a low impact in variation since this spread shall be constant per scenario.
- The time buckets are considered at their mid-point (not weighted which is another simplification) or at their maturity point (which may generate wrong effects in case of curve in backwardation for example).

---

[20] The choice of the "continuous" exponential discount factor is not justified. We believe that the national regulator will not make an issue of banks using classical actuarial interest rates. This is an example of undue technicality in regulation.

- The actualized value of the cash flows is then calculated per currency and per scenario.
- There is <u>one reference scenario which is the current rate curve</u>, that is without taking into account the forward (another weakness) <u>and 6 stressed scenarios</u>:
    - 2 translations: Parallel up and down
    - A steepener and a flattener
    - 1 scenario short rates up and one short rates down

Automatic IR options are calculated MtM per scenario, with an increase in volatility of 25% in the stressed scenarios[21]. The perimeter is global, even though there may be some flexibility for non micro-hedging derivatives (point 131).

EVE by currency is equal to the sum of the actualized CF (in the currency) and MtM of options:

$$EVE_{currency} = \sum DF_t . CF_t + MTM_{options}$$

The variation of EVE by currency is equal to the difference between the EVE of the base scenario and the EVE in one of the six scenarios:

$$\Delta EVE_{scenario\ i, currency} = EVE_{scenario\ base, currency} - EVE_{scenario\ i, currency}$$

The standardized EVE risk measure is equal to the worst variation taking into account only the currencies for which the variation is negative:

$$\text{Standardized EVE risk measure}^{22} = \max_{i \in \{1,2...,6\}} \left(\sum_{c \text{ such as } \Delta EVE_c \geq 0} fx_c . \Delta EVE_c \right)$$

---

[21] Page 29-130.1 the rule requires to deduct the premium received, which means that banks need to keep the data or reverse engineer it. However, since this should be a constant and we focus on the variation of value, we do not understand why the text includes it...

[22] The formula in the Basel document is unnecessarily complex including the maximum between 0 and positive numbers. It has been simplified. We added an FX rate because without it, it would make no sense.

So there is no compensation between net long and short positions between two currencies.

The different scenarios are summarized in the following table, knowing that:

- The base scenario is the current IR curve,
- Regulators can set up IR floor at 0 or below
- Shock shall be reviewed every 5 years. They are currently calculated as a weighted average of past observations from 2000 to 2015 with a floor at 100 bps and cap at 500 bps for short term, 400 bps for parallel and 300 bp for long-term.

Scenario (t in year)	Parallel up	Parallel down	steepener	flattener	Short rate up	Short rate down
Parameter ρ €	+2%	-2%	ρ_{short} -2.5% / ρ_{Long} +1%	ρ_{short} +2.5% / ρ_{Long} -1%	ρ_{short} +2.5%	ρ_{short} -2.5%
$\Delta r(t)$ formula	+ ρ	+ ρ	$0,65 \cdot \rho_{short} \cdot e^{-t/4} + 0,9 \cdot \rho_{long} \cdot (1 - e^{-t/4})$	$0,65 \cdot \rho_{short} \cdot e^{-t/4} + 0,9 \cdot \rho_{long} \cdot (1 - e^{-t/4})$	+ $\rho_{short} \cdot e^{-t/4}$	+ $\rho_{short} \cdot e^{-t/4}$
$\Delta r(t)$ for €	+2%	-2%	$-0,65 \cdot 2,5\% \cdot e^{-t/4} + 0,9 \cdot 1\% \cdot (1 - e^{-t/4})$	$0,65 \cdot 2,5\% \cdot e^{-t/4} - 0,9 \cdot 1\% \cdot (1 - e^{-t/4})$	$+2,5\% \cdot e^{-t/4}$	$-2,5\% \cdot e^{-t/4}$
CPR assets			Min(1, $\gamma_{scenario} \cdot CPR_{portfolio}$)			
γ_{assets}	0.8	1.2	0.8	1.2	0.8	1.2
$\Gamma_{deposits}$	1.2	0.8	0.8	1.2	1.2	0.8

Variation of NIM

The regulator doesn't set up a limit in term of duration of modeling and just requires to disclose the effect on the first 12 months (even though it recommends to do calculation over 3 years), that is a small part of the issue since balance sheet on average requires about 5 years to get renewed. It requests also to perform only the two translation scenarios under the assumption of a constant balance sheet ("roll at 100%"). This is clearly insufficient since impacts are most visible with moves above 200 bp and CPR clearly higher than 120% of the original ones during the wave of prepayments. Finally, notice the concern of the regulator that "earnings based measure do not necessarily identify the risks to capital that can arise from revaluation of AFS portfolio" (since AFS moves don't impact NIM but

OCI): this is the reason why we always recommend to model the full balance sheet and incomes statement.

Some general comments

IRRBB is still part of pillar 2

The regulator hesitated to impose a pillar 1 ratio and gave up for technical reasons, considering situations were not homogeneous enough. It also did not want to add an undue additional capital requirement in the current environment except for establishments clearly significantly exposed to an interest rate risk. The question this assertion raises is if IRRBB shall stay in pillar 2 or if, in a second step, the regulator shall move it into pillar 1.

Actually, the regulatory IRRBB calculation requirement is de facto similar to a pillar 1 approach, with a ratio to respect, a standard methodology and an advanced approach. In time, banks will adapt and the first argument against pillar 1 shall vanish.

Indeed, imposing a capital requirement in front of this risk below the current threshold would be simple. However, as of today, few banks were hit by direct IR mismanagement in such a way that they collapsed totally, out of the Savings and Loans crisis[23]. But many were hit in significant ways, even though the losses remained often confidential. In addition, the current environment is a real concern. With most of their assets insensitive to IR (the current accounts and in a certain way some savings accounts), commercial banks shall see their Net Interest Margin ("NIM") under massive pressure, should the current negative rates environment last. They shall react by expanding their balance sheet but, with the quantitative easing and the lack of growth pushing the spreads down, with liquidity being so cheap, balance sheets will weaken and one can expect some "accidents".

What we anticipate is rather a two-step approach: with this text, the regulator requires banks to put in place the adequate modeling systems. In a second step, it shall imagine other scenarios, than the 6 ones mentioned,

---

[23] The S&L were refunding short-term long-term loans. When the Reagan administration freed IR, short-term rates soared and the S&L embarked into a strategy of expansion of their balance sheet to generate new revenues through the acquisition of junk bonds.

more directly related to our current environment. And while remaining in pillar 2, it may require additional actions to mitigate risk. By doing so, regulators will simply stick to the recommendations of the Basel committee. Indeed, the text explicitly states that regulators have broad freedom to (1) expand the regulation to smaller banks and (2) define additional parameters to identify "outlier banks", that is banks with excessive interest rates exposure.

Banks have indeed nowadays no choice than to restructure and reduce their cost. In parallel, they must improve technology and expertise to set up lighter financial teams that are technically stronger.

IRRBB is finally acknowledged as a major risk in banking

Bankers believed before the crisis that only market risk and credit risk could push down their houses. With the crisis, they discovered that liquidity risk was as well deadly: Dexia was refunding more than 40% of its very long-term assets at less than 3 months, Bear Stearns[24] and Lehman were also too short of liquidity...

With the negative IR, they are actually discovering long-term damage of the IRRBB. But already in the past, many institutions were hit by IRRBB: the savings and loans crisis is the quintessential example of the collapse of a group of banks which were refunding long term assets at short term rates[25]. Other examples of IRRBB losses are less known but are as consistent and damaging[26].

---

[24] Bear was long subprime when it collapsed. The trigger was its $30bn stock of Freddie Mac and Fannie Mae bonds. As one of the top market maker on this $5 trillion market, the size of the stock was not huge. However, when market value when down by 10%, the NAV of the bank fell to zero. Its refunding was too short. Two key hedge funds decided to transfer their assets in custody, around $20bn, which was enough to generate a default of payment.

[25] When the Reagan administration free the short term rates and subsequently these ones jumped, they had no choice than to embark into a strategy of expansion of their balance sheet in order to compensate the collapsing of their NIM: the savings and loans didn't have the commercial opportunity to do so, so they bought junk bonds until these ones collapsed.

[26] Most files remained confidential but losses have been regularly massive. The last public ALM error concerned the $6.2 billion losses of the JPM London office. However, the loss was not related to an IR move but rather regarded a macro-position on CDS.

The regulator finally acknowledges the interest rate risk structural to the banking activity as "excessive IRRBB can pose a significant threat to bank's current capital base and/or future earnings if not managed appropriately" (page 3 §8).

Components of interest rates

The annex includes a decomposition of client rate in 5 components:

1. Risk free rate on the maturity
2. A market duration spread defined as part of the additional spread relating to duration only. Practically, this is challenging to calculate.
3. A market liquidity spread which is supposed to correct for the difference in balance between buyers and sellers of the specific duration (a distortion on the RFR!).
4. A general market credit spread: that is the part of the spread charged for the market credit risk (not liquidity nor balance between buyers and sellers but including a risk margin)
5. The idiosyncratic credit spread which includes also a risk margin.

The text considers these components as "more readily identifiable in traded instruments". Even on a liquid market, this sounds challenging to quantify and rather theoretical. However, the analysis of the different factors is relevant and introduces the notion of internal rate of cession (IRC) implicitly in the ALM approach.

It also expresses the importance of credit spread risk in the banking book (CSRBB) which "needs to be monitored and assess"[27].

Improving the standardized framework.

The standardized framework does not appear as a heavy simplification versus more sophisticated modeling. It captures already almost all the

---

[27] The regulator emphasizes the complexity of the evolution of the credit spread. Cf "pricing of bonds with risk premium, market value versus economic value", ALM-Vision, March 2016.

IRRBB. A higher sophistication should not bring much more but would probably clarify the process. Actually, what else could have a more accurate framework?

- Smaller steps: the 19 times bucket are a false simplification since banks will still have to gather data. Smaller buckets make more sense because in ALM the most expensive work is data collection. Using small steps shall allow banks to use this data not only for ALM but also for budget, business plan and capital planning. We have always recommended monthly steps because smaller steps (daily) would not bring any additional useful accuracy for a risk developing progressively. Still monthly steps will allow avoiding estimations of average buckets for not a very expensive additional data treatment.
- Automatic embedded options (loans with caps, floors…) should be integrated for their intrinsic value into the NIM calculation even for ΔEVE. It would provide a more accurate view. The time value variation can then be calculated separately as it is done in solvency 2.
- The cap on CPR at 100% is not a drama for the current defined scenarios. However, last IR move (2015) resulted in CPR above 100% for one month for some portfolio of our customers (keep in mind that CPR is annualized, a CPR at 120% over one month means that 10% of the portfolio was renegotiated).
- The use of the forward curve as base scenario would give a more accurate estimate of the future NIM.
- The regulation does not go beyond the NIM[28] whereas the 2005 text clearly included commissions as IR sensitive. Answering the key question of the top management "what shall be the impact of this scenario on my incomes and capital" requires to integrate the AFS and MtM effects linked to the IR also. This is all the more important that

---

[28] Even though page 37 it mentions "the impact of any fees collected/paid for exercise of options".

the LCR pushed banks to build up big portfolios of liquidity, often put in AFS. Obviously integrating AFS impact in earnings-based approach has always been a necessity[29].

- Treasury on the net position for the EVE isn't taken into account whereas coupons and spreads are to be included. This is obviously a strong assumption assuming that treasury shall be always available at the actualization curve price.
- A bond with a coupon at CMS 5 Years resetting every 3 months is considered as a three months maximum fixed rate bond. That is assuming that CMS 5 Years indexed bonds are valued at par at each time of reset. This is obviously an approximation[30], most of the time acceptable but not always. Only bonds with coupons equal to the forward rate of the concerned period of reset calculated using the same actualization curve are equal to par at each reset date.

A more fundamental disappointment in this regulation is that the regulator still sticks with the static gap methodology with its net position per time bucket. It would have been much easier to request a simulation of the variation of market value of the balance sheet under the 6 scenarios' assumptions of run-off. The result would have been more accurate, integrating treasury effects, easier to understand, easier to explain for the same amount of work required. Indeed, it is more complicated for an institution to implement the rules of truncation for variable rates bonds, with separation of the spread than to simply reprice them. And results would be better. Notice that institutions are allowed to do so but obviously, they may feel less confident in front of their regulator.

Indeed, if one considers the value of a set of cash flows to be their actualized sum. The new static gap methodology requires to sum the CF per period

---

[29] Indeed the assertion page 43 saying that "last but not least, earnings-based measures do not necessarily identify the risks to capital that can arise from revaluation of AFS portfolios" is the denunciation of a weakness we have observed in main banks.

[30] CMS bonds even include a convexity effect and so a sensitivity to volatility.

and then actualize them whereas a "Marked to model" methodology would require to actualize the CF of a line and then sum them, which is absolutely identical!

$$\underbrace{\sum_t \beta_t \cdot \left[\sum_{lines} CF_{line}(t) \right]}_{\text{static gap methodology}} = \underbrace{\sum_{lines} \left[\sum_t \beta_t \cdot CF_{line}(t) \right]}_{\text{marked to model methodology}}$$

This fact is even more obvious that the text requires to price the options too. It only stops short requiring to price the very complex prepayment options[31].

Notice than it would be easier for a bank starting from scratch its ALM system to simply re-price MtM the derivatives (swaps) instead of having to integrate them into the gap methodology. Still, most banks had already in place some kind of static gap analysis and the regulator tried to simply expand the previous methodology to its new requirement. This raises the strategic question for a bank of adapting its current systems or simply redoing one new.

The variation of economic value is still neither an indicator of the sensitivity of the incomes statement to an IR variation nor of the variation of value of the bank.

The motivation of the regulator to stick on the static methodology is well known:

1. It is an approach matching its concern: if an institution is in difficulty and the regulator has to step in and take control of the institution in order to wind down the assets and liabilities, it wants to avoid a major loss. Under this hypothesis, there shall be no significant new activity and it is logical for the regulator to focus on the existing balance sheet only, making sure its variation of value remain reasonable.

---

[31] Cf "modeling and pricing prepayments: a market approach", ALM-Vision papers, June 2016

2. The new production modeling raises more uncertainty in term of volume and prices and regulators don't want to enter into endless discussion[32] with managements about what they may achieve commercially tomorrow.
3. The static approach seems to better match the new fashion of the so-called "marked to market". This trend is still very strong despite the numerous articles criticizing its assumptions (absence of arbitrage opportunities, liquidity, short selling...) or describing the disappearing of the market during the crisis.

Still it faces several weaknesses.

Duration convention on NMD still conducts to underestimate the IRRBB in most commercial banks.

The first weakness is obviously on the conventions on assets without defined maturity, mainly the current accounts and savings accounts. Assuming an "interest rate amortizing convention" for current accounts is equivalent to defining a sensitivity of current accounts to the interest rates.

The regulator provides a cap on Non Maturity Deposits ("NMD"). Its goal is to get a homogeneous methodology between banks, which is legitimate. However, this methodology under-estimate the exposure to IR and inversely over-estimate the impact of an IR shock on the liquidation value of the stock in the balance sheet of the bank (we will call it Value In Force – VIF- by analogy with insurance business).

Let take the classical simple example of a bank with 100 of NMD funding an annual production of 20 of bullet loans with 5 years[33] of initial duration. At equilibrium, the bank has 100 as stable assets[34] with an average duration of 2.51 years (at 5% flat interest rate).

---

[32] This point is expressly written in footnote 9 page 8.

[33] This example seems very simple but actually it is a good rough simplification of the position of most retail banks, if you add in addition some short-term deposits.

[34] 20 at 5 years, 20 at 4 years (coming from the previous year's production), 20 at 3 years, 20 at 2 years and 20 at 1 year.

- If the bank assumes a linear amortizing over 5 years of its NMD, it has no gap and subsequently no EVE exposure (out of the spread) to IR,
- If the bank assumes a linear amortizing over less than 5 years of its NMD, it is in risk in case of increase of the interest rates in term of NIM. In term of EVE, it is at risk in case of decrease of interest rates (but the result is an underestimation).
- If the bank assumes a linear amortizing over five years of its NMD, it is in risk in case of decrease of the interest rate in term of NIM, but since average duration is capped at 5 years, it still underestimates its risk. In term of EVE, it is in risk in case of increase of the IR but here again the result is underestimated.

The true answer in stable regime (renewal of the balance sheet by rolling at 100%) is that every decrease of the IR by 100 basis points shall reduce the NIM progressively over 5 years by 100 bps (20 bps per year).

In case of increase of the IR by 100 bp, the MtM of the loan portfolio shall go down by -2.5%, a loss for the liquidator, since deposits shall be simply reimbursed at par.

The regulatory approach to Economic Value is not considering the risk of the bank in going concern but the opposite risk of the regulator in case of liquidation.

Indeed, the previous example shows clearly that the scenarios generating a loss are different between MtM of the stock and variation of incomes in going concern.

The text gives a clear definition of the EVE: "EVE measures the theoretical change in the net present value of the balance sheet excluding equity. The measure therefore depicts the change in equity value resulting from an interest rate shock". The regulatory approach is not taking into account the risk of the bank in going concern but the risk of the regulator in case it has to liquidate the portfolio. However here also it shall provide a false estimate of the true liquidating value since in liquidation, NMD are worth simply the par and the IR shock only impact the loan book. Indeed, the reality of our example is that if interest rates are going down, the value of the loan book shall appreciate instantaneously but the new production will be done at a lower rate, which shall impact progressively the value of the bank. Inversely if IR are going up, the value of the stock shall depreciate but progressively, the stock will disappear and the new production will be generated at better rate.

Indeed, the new regulation did not abandon the wrong model for NMD and the calculation is not going to give to regulators a true estimate of its risk: its real risk would be to assume that NMD are interest rates insensitive (or do the exact sensitivity calculation). It is to the advantage of most of the banks to choose a duration of deposits at the allowed maximum since it shall reduce their capital requirement.

We do not speak here about liquidity. Amortizing convention of NMD is absolutely relevant for liquidity management, representing the target reinvestment strategy the bank choose (as "cautious and reasonable") for reinvesting its deposits.

Conceptually, value of NMD is intrinsically linked to the market value of a bank

Formally, the stable part of NMD can be seen as perpetual liabilities[35] with a cost c, which can be correlated with IR and isn't null since there are always cost of collecting NMD (banks provide account management services through internet and phone platforms and branches for the brick and mortar players). Price is therefore in a flat IR environment with positive rate r:

$$P(c,r) = \lim_{n} \left[\sum_{t=1}^{n} \frac{c}{(1+r)^t} + \frac{1}{(1+r)^n} \right] = \lim_{n} \left[\frac{c}{r} + \frac{1}{(1+r)^n} \cdot \left(1 - \frac{c}{r}\right) \right] = \frac{c}{r}$$

- If c=r, P=100%. The bank has no advantage to collect NMD.
- If c<r, P<100%. The NMD being registered at 100% in the liabilities of the bank, this one enjoys an underlying profit on deposit activity. This is the normal model.

---

[35] Current accounts are M1 and M1 is moving like inflation plus an additional parameter depending on the speed of circulation of currency and the IR.

- If c>r, P>100%. This situation, which may be the case currently, translates the fact that then NMD are more expensive for the bank than market long term resources.
- Obviously, r<0 generates an infinite price for deposit.
- C=0 gives P=0. A free resource for the bank.

Actually, the price doesn't matter. What matters is the sensitivity of the price to r: $-\dfrac{\partial \ln P}{\partial r} = \dfrac{1}{r}$ which is much higher than defined by the regulation. However, since NMD are not value MtM in the balance sheet, this sensitivity has no direct impact on the value in force of the business.

In our example, let us assume that loans are made at 5% and cost/incomes ratio is 50%, cost of risk 0.5 point, SCR 10%, risk free rate is at 3% flat.

- Before IR shock, the bank generates 5% - 50%.5% -0.5% = 2% incomes per year and ROE is 20%, that is 17 points above long term rates.
- After IR shock, incomes decrease each years by 0.2 pts to 1% incomes per year (in year 5) and ROE is 10%, that is only 8 point above long term rates.

It is difficult to anticipate the impact on the market value of the bank but assuming a constant PER of 10, before shock the bank is worth 20 that is a goodwill of 10 ; after the shock (after 5 years) it is worth 10 that is at book value. This very simple example explains part of the mechanisms on current valuation of banks[36].

If the regulator was going to take over the institution and put it in run-off, after the shock, it shall have to liquidate a portfolio of loans of duration 2.5 made 100 bps above market. It would generate a profit of +2.5. The value of NMD would have reduced significantly from their high valuation (let assume c=1.5 pts then P=50 before shock that is an underlying profit of 50 and P=75 that is an underlying profit of 25 after shock). But the regulator

---

[36] Currently, other phenomena are impacting the valuation of banks: higher capital needs, global decrease of the risk premium on equity following the quantitative easing...

still would simply reimburse the deposit at par in case of liquidation generating a final profit of +2.5.

If it finds a bank to buy the deposits, it would generate a profit of 27.5 instead of 50 before the shock assuming the buyer prices the deposits at their real value. In reality, no buyer would invest above its market PER. A market value of a deposit collection activity without a loan book (and capital) would rather be 15 before shock and 5 after. But again, this is a free option for the regulator. Inversely, in case of increase of the interest rates, obviously the bank would be in better shape but for the regulator having to step in, the liquidation of the loan book would generate a loss.

A simple example – key figures	Before shock	5 years after IR down 1%	5 years after IR up 1%
Risk free rate	3%	2%	4%
Loan rate	5%	4%	6%
Total balance sheet	100	100	100
Capital (assumed no return on capital, no IR risk)	10	10	10
Net Interest Margin (out of capital investment)	5	4	6
Costs (C/I = 50%)	-2.5	-2.5 (unchanged)	-2.5
Risk	-0.5	-0.5	-0.5
Incomes before tax	**2**	**1**	**3**
Market cap. PER=10 unchanged	20	10	30
PBV	2	1	3
Revenues on reinvesting NMD at RFR	3	2	4
Cost of collecting NMD	-1.5	-1.5	-1.5
Incomes made on NMD	**1.5**	**0.5**	**2.5**
Value of NMD under formula c/r	50	75	37.5
Value of NMD priced with PER=10	15	5	25
Incomes made on loan activity	**0.5**	**0.5**	**0.5**
Value of loan book	100	102.5 just after shock	97.5 just after shock
Value of loan activity with PER=10	5	5	5
Economic value if NMD linear 5 years	10	10	10
Economic value if NMD linear 3 years	10	10.73	9.27
Economic value if NMD linear 7 years	10	9.37	10.63

Conclusion

The April 2016 D368 Basel regulation is a revolution in the sense that it shall finally impose the best practices inside banks in term of ALM. The text unfortunately suffers from unnecessary technicity and one can regret that the regulator did not go one step further[37]. However, it faces every key issue in ALM modeling and finally acknowledges the importance for banks to balance both approaches: variation of EVE and variation of NIM.

The timing of implementation is very ambitious and banks should react quickly first to train their staff and second to build the required data.

---

[37] It is our opinion that a tidying-up of the text shall take place in a couple of years.

The NEW STANDARD for IRRBB:
UNDERSTANDING the complementarity of approaches in estimating the variation in Economic Value of Equity (EVE) and the sensitivity of Net Interest Margin (NIM) – a CASE STUDY

Introduction

The April 2016 Basel Committee directive d368 *"Interest Rate Risk in the Banking Book"* ("IRRBB") translates into the regulation the necessity of implementing a dual approach between the static valuation of the existing balance sheet (the "EVE") and the modeling of Net Interest Margin ("NIM") through a dynamic approach.

This d368 directive seeks to avoid a repeat of the mistakes of the past, which were observed with the use of the simple "static gap" analysis method. It is fundamental to understand the significance of the two methodologies, their complementarity and the motivation of the regulator. It is the only way to implement a proper Asset and Liability Management (ALM) strategy, to adapt limits to the characteristics of each institution, and to avoid some major errors.

D368 enters into effect by January 2018. Therefore, institutions have only 12 months to implement the new regulation. This is a short amount of time compared to the massive work of modeling and documentation that the new regulation requires.

Static versus dynamic gaps

Up to recently, ALM was often divided into two schools of thought: the school pushing for static gaps and the school of thought pushing for dynamic gaps:

- Proponents of the **dynamic gap** approach simulate the balance sheet and income statements by taking into account the new production of loans and by assuming steady business activity for the bank for years to come. Proponents of this approach consider the analysis to be closer reality. They further adopt the view that it is the only approach that provides an answer to management's core question "if interest rates shift by X% and projections of the business plan in terms of production and deposit collection are met, by how much income will be affected?"

- Proponents of static gap approach consider the methodology used by **dynamic gap** to be built on too many assumptions. A bank's balance sheet is commonly and almost always entirely renewed after five years. The efficiency of the dynamic gap methodology is further questioned by adherents of the static gap method due to the complexity of its implementation. Indeed, the renewal of each credit line results in the production of new loans that have each their own amortization schedule. Proponents of **static** gap analysis assume that since future loan production is unknown, it does not have to be taken into account. They consider that it can be hedged at a later stage. Proponents of this approach operate in a "compartmentalized bank" approach and define a convention of amortization for deposits without maturity (mainly current accounts). Proponents of dynamic gap analysis criticize static gap analysis for being far removed from reality as well as for transferring part of interest rate risk from loan production onto commercial business lines. It also disapproves of the static gap methodology because of inaccurate liquidity analysis, excessive arbitrary use of amortization conventions and inaccurate interest rate risk analysis methodology.

However, the two methods can be reconciled in a simple manner. To reconcile them, one needs to process new business separately. This way, the effects of reinvestments, of new business growth, and of the potential new reinvestment assumptions can be defined and monitored separately. The lack of activation of new business gives rise to "gross" static gaps, that is to say static gaps before any convention on the disposal of assets or of liabilities of indefinite duration. Static gap analysis allows for an initial insight into liquidity risk whereas dynamic gap anlysis provides an opportunity to anticipate reinvestment risk (yield / interest rate, spread...).

We get the standard static gap analysis by fixing runoff conventions for indefinite term assets or liabilities. This analysis can then be completed with dynamic analysis by using the reinvestment rules for new business from funds of indefinite term.

Static gap analysis does differentiate between yield gaps and liquidity gaps. It is thus possible to reconcile the two methods. This requires discipline in modeling it. It can become quite a complex if one takes into account the whole evolution of the balance sheet:

- Liabilities that run off according to conventions - for instance current accounts - must roll over onto themselves (that is to say that fall-off is reinvested into a new production of the same product) so that stock progress can be traced when outstanding amortization of new business is taken into account.
- In interest rate gaps, floating assets and liabilities are removed after the renewal of the coupon. Also, a quarterly floating rate credit duration of 24 months should be modeled just as a 3 months fixed credit rate that is replaced by a new 21 months loan at floating rate, a model that is heavy in terms of implementation.
- In liquidity gap analysis, one must not roll over floating rates in a manner that is different to rolling over fixed interest rates.

We get static gaps by freezing new business. By integrating new business to the model, the hold on new business is lifted and we get dynamic gap analysis. Liquidity and yield effects on these rollovers are clearly different to stock run-off. The concept may seem somewhat abstract.

In a certain way, the new D368 regulation closes the debate between the proponents of one or the other of these two schools since it now requires both[38]. As we mentioned, this does not mean that we have to develop two different systems as we will see in the following example.

A simple example

For clarity of explanation, we take the example of a very conventional bank, observed almost everywhere across the world. We then develop this example using both methodologies.

The retail bank has the following characteristics:

Assets	amount	duration	Rate	Liabilities	amount	duration	Rate
Treasury & investments	8,000	0.5	E3M+0.1%	Current accounts	30,000	no maturity	0
Fixed rate loans	60,000	4	CMS+1%	Savings accounts	20,000	no maturity	6 month average E3M - 0.1% with floor at 0.05%
Variable rate loans	30,000	2	E3M+1%	Short-term times deposit	20,000	0.25	E3M - 0.05%
immobilization	2,000	no maturity	0	Issuances	20,000	1.7 (5Y linear)	Fixed rate, new issuances at CMS 5Y + 0.2%
Total assets	100,000			Capital	10,000	no maturity	0
				Total liabilities	100,000		

It has a simple balance sheet, focused on its customer banking business. The proportion between long-term mortgage loans, equipment loans and short-term loans was chosen, in order to represent as much as possible most of the retail banks in Europe. Indeed, retail banks in Europe are characterized by limited corporate business and significant mortgage activity.

We also initially assume that there is no business growth and that the bank simply renews its balance sheet (which is the assumption of the regulator under IRRBB d368). We will then later see the impact of growth of assets and liabilities (which sometimes is key).

Assets

The main activity of the bank is to produce loans, mostly mortgages at fixed rate. The rest of its activity consists of variable rate loans: treasury loans,

---

[38] We were one of the first to emphasize the complementarity of both approaches, cf "modélisation de gestion financière d'une banque commerciale", S. Moulin, 2012, ALM-Vision.

consumer loans, equipment loans. The proportion is relatively conventional, close to what is observed in most of the countries.

Of course, the bank also has some fixed assets: premises, material...

Liabilities

Like every retail bank, its main source of funding is customers' current and savings accounts. Savings accounts bear interest at a proxy of the average of the 6 last months observed Euribor 3 Month interest rate (E3M) with a floor at 15 basis points (bp), minus 10 basis points of commercial margin. In the current European context, this floor is key[39]. Even though rates on savings accounts are defined by the banks themselves, they usually can not be negative if current accounts are not also invoiced. In our simulations, we reach the floor. This means that these savings account will not reprice for a decrease in interest rates (IR). But they would reprice in case of an increase in IR.

In addition, the bank pays a little more than E3M to get some time deposits and it uses its stock of mortgages as collateral to issue covered bonds. Actually, it is a well-capitalized bank.

First qualitative analysis: the bank is exposed to a decrease in Interest Rates (IR).

It is fundamental in ALM to begin with a qualitative analysis of the balance sheet and income statement. Far from being a waste of time, it provides key insights on the exposures of the bank.

Effect of an IR move on the Net Interest Margin (NIM)

Simply by observing the structure of the balance sheet in our example, it is clear that if interest rates decrease, the NIM of the bank will be under stress:

- 38 000 in assets at E3M and 40 000 in liabilities will adjust, giving a small profit to the bank if savings accounts are not at their floor.

---

[39] In France, most popular savings accounts get an IR defined by the government with a target of inflation plus 0 or 25 bp. However, during the crisis, the government did not follow the rule and left the IR at 75 bp far above its theoretical limit.

However, if they are at their floor, the net exposure is around 18 000 and the bank is exposed to a decrease in IR also on its assets and liabilities at variable rate.
- More importantly, the new production of loans on the massive fixed rate loans portfolio will be affected. The first few years, the issuances having also to renew, the blow will be slightly compensated but it will then gradually develop into what is referred to as the "Noria effect[40]", on a massive scale.
- Symmetrically, there is no impact in term of income statement on the current accounts and since they pay no interest (there may be an indirect impact in case of variation of volumes of the current accounts, due to arbitrages between M1 and M2, as observed in big IR moves).

Inversely, if interest rates increase, the bank will face a slight loss on its variable assets since savings accounts will reprice. Yet, the Noria effect will gradually prevail and generate increased NIM, even though customers' loans prices are reacting slower than swap rates.

If the curve flattens, the NIM will gradually be affected: the 60 000 of fixed rate loans will progressively reprice whereas only the 20 000 issuances will adjust in the liabilities.

Indeed, our example is typical and the bank is conventionally exposed to:

- A decrease in interest rates,
- A flattening of the yield curve,
- The time lag of adjustment of assets and liabilities,
- The correlation risks between IR and customers' behaviors (for both assets and liabilities, but mainly on the asset side for IR, the liability side is mostly for liquidity risk and moves are usually less massive)

---

[40] We call Noria effect the gradual renewal of the loan books with new loans produced at new market conditions. These new loans progressively impact the revenues of the book, each new one adding to the previous ones.

Effect on the Net Asset Value (NAV) and market value of the bank

Obviously, if the NIM is decreasing, the market value of the bank will also be under pressure. To value a bank, investors look traditionally at two elements:

- The Price Earnings Ratio (P/E Ratio or PER): with the NIM going down, the income of the bank will be under stress and assuming a constant PER, its market value will decease.
- The Price to Book ratio (P/B ratio or PB ratio): this indicator uses a book value that is not valuing each line of the balance sheet marked to market. Subsequently, an interest rate shift that does not generate an accounting loss in the books of a bank does not affect instantly its book value. And the PB ratio is usually decreasing because of the impact on the income, and therefore on the price of the bank.

However, for the regulator, the vision is different. Imagine that the regulator takes over the management of the bank in order to unwind it (for a reason that is unrelated to the IR situation). Its main issue will be to sell the fixed rate loans book and the customer deposits.

- If interest rates are going down just after the regulator takes over the bank, the fixed rate loans book will see its price increase. Inversely, if interest rates are going up, the price of the fixed rate loans book will decrease.
- The price of savings accounts will be relatively stable due to the savings accounts being indexed on E3M. Only the current accounts will be a challenge for the unwinding regulator: obviously, if these accounts represent real customers, there will be banks to buy them with a premium. If the IR are going up, the value of the current accounts will go up and the potential buyer will be ready to pay more. Inversely, if IR are going down, their value will shrink. But if, for any reason, there is no buyer, the regulator will just have to give their money back to the depositors and ask them to transfer their accounts to another bank.

For the regulator, the exposure of the bank will highly depend on the value of the current accounts. At worse, if it just has to pay back their money to the customers, the liquidator will be at risk of an increase in interest rates. In case of central bank intervention, this scenario is obviously very likely considering that the bank just faced such a dramatic situation that the regulator had to step in (usually regulators step in only in case of a run to the bank[41]).

In a "normal" situation (that is without a run to the bank), the regulator will be at risk in case of a decrease in interest rates. In both cases, the regulator seeks to minimize its risk and the one of its shareholders, the country's people.

Duration and modeling of the fixed rate loans book of a commercial bank

Regulation d368 IRRBB point IV paragraph 11.5 defines a cap on the average maturity of core deposits between 5 years (retail/transactional) and 4 years (wholesale). Some bankers expressed concern that this figure was too low to allow for a reasonable ALM management.

Actually, this kind of convention is obviously not the result of some econometric model on current and savings accounts (because current accounts are the core of the monetary mass M1 and as a stock with constant input and output, they can not be modelled in run-down. Historically M1 has always been growing, outperforming inflation by 2 to 4 points depending on IR and on the velocity of money). <u>The convention is a target in term of reinvestment and, from a regulator point of view, a conventional value of core deposits.</u>

Therefore the question is rather whether or not this convention matches the characteristics of the current assets of European banks.

Let us assume a bank producing every year 100 of 20 years constant monthly payments on loans, with 5% constant prepayment rate (CPR). Interest rate paid on loans is 2.5% at market price. After 20 years, its stock

---

[41] A run to the bank refers to a situation where customers withdraw massively their assets, following the announcement of a situation which they consider to be seriously jeopardizing the safety of their money.

would be stable, with an outstanding nominal of 9 480 and the duration of the stock would be of 5.3 years (initial duration of a loan is 6.9 years).

Obviously, for lower initial duration and/or higher CPR, the duration of the stock would be lower.

Modified duration (in years) of a stock of constant monthly loans payments produced regularly (constant stock)

CPR \ initial duration	20	15	12	Portfolio composed of 50% of 20Y / 40% of 15Y / 10% of 12Y
3%	5.6	4.5	3.7	5.0
4%	5.5	4.4	3.6	4.8
5%	5.3	4.3	3.5	4.7
6%	5.1	4.2	3.5	4.6
7%	5.0	4.1	3.4	4.5
8%	4.8	4.0	3.3	4.3
Loan rate	2.5%	2.3%	2.1%	2.38%

A bank usually offers mortgage loans of initial duration between 12 years and 20 years. Under reasonable market conditions, <u>its mortgage book should have naturally a duration of around 5 years</u>, slightly lower if interest rates are higher (duration decreases when IR increase – see the example of the portfolio above).

Actually, <u>this means that the regulator allows banks to refund their mortgage books with core deposits</u> (from an IR point of view, the liquidity exposure being defined through its adequate limits). This is a very powerful result and clearly shows that banks should not worry about this limit set by the regulator. Indeed, it sounds reasonable to limit excessive transformation that is above 20 years. Furthermore, considering the fact that loans books of banks have also a significant portion of shorter-term loans<u>, the requirement sounds very reasonable and is not really a constraint</u>.

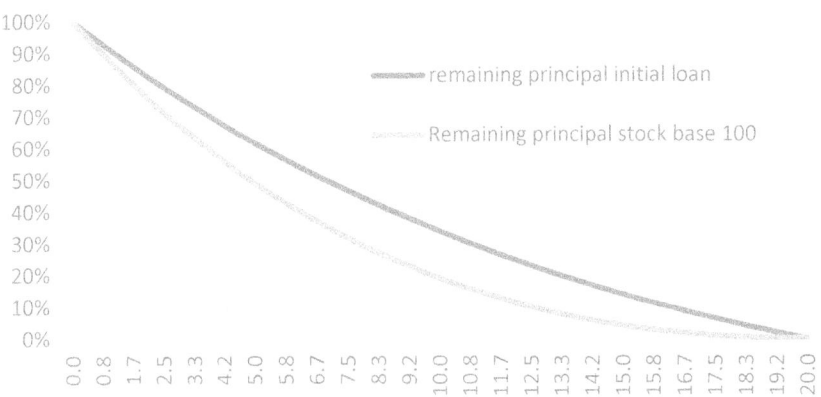

It is very interesting to look at the stock amortization curve. Most institutions still use linear convention of amortization of their current accounts, sometimes adding a 3 years bullet period. Actually, using the natural curve of the loans' book would allow naturally to get a static gap hedged position, especially for a long-term bucket.

Furthermore, this inversed exponential curve has the great advantage of being stable, it is even the only shape of amortization[42] where the amortization of the stock matches the amortization of the new loans production[43], which justifies its use it for no maturity deposits (NMD).

This point is important since banks sometimes define limits per bucket. The longest buckets are pretty sensitive to conventions and a linear convention

---

[42] Cf Antoine Frachot, Paul Demey, Gael Riboulet « méthodologie de gestion actif-passif bancaire », groupe de recherche opérationelle, Crédit Lyonnais, janvier 2003, chap. 4.3.3
[43] Finally, the nominal of the stock is equal to the modified duration of the initial loan, c.f. "modeling and pricing prepayments", ALM-Vision research papers, June 2016

may generate swings in the longest buckets, even beyond limits. Obviously, these over-limits have to be analyzed in a very cautious manner because most of the time they are just the result of conventions. In general, it is recommended to hedge properly the 3 following years, to have acceptable hedge from year 3 to 5 (the duration of the balance sheet) and then some remaining position from year 7 to year 10. The longer buckets have only to be analyzed to make sure that there is no massive issue to address. If not, then no action should be taken[44] since they ca not be justified objectively and may expose the bank to major risks.

Another important element linked to the natural curve of the constant monthly payment loans is the fact that a significant portion of the loans amortize the following year: here more than 10% the first year. This fact is often forgotten whereas it means that the "Noria" effect is pretty fast with 50% of the balance sheet renewing before 5 years.

---

[44] This means that very long term positions, especially through forward swaps, are most of the time a complete non-sense and cannot objectively qualify as macro-hedging. In our example, they would be just highly leveraged speculative positions.

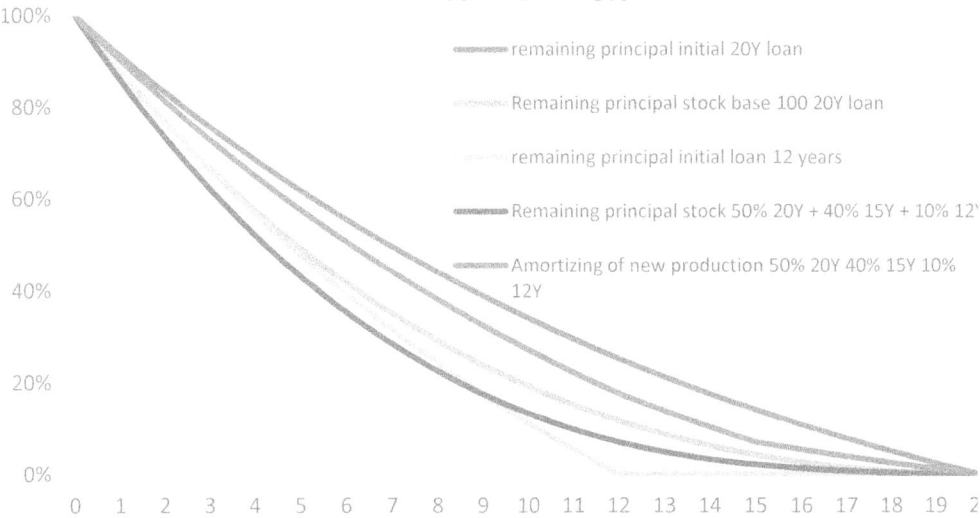

In addition, the bank's loan books include consumer and equipment loans, which have shorter duration. We assume a portfolio generated evenly each year with 5% prepayments made of:
- 30% of 10 years linear loans,
- 50% of 5 years linear loans,
- 20% of 3 years linear loans.

Duration of the linear loans book – equipment loans

CPR \ initial duration	10	5	3	Portfolio 30%/50%/20%
3%	3.08	1.64	1.03	1.95
4%	3.03	1.63	1.02	1.93
5%	2.98	1.62	1.02	1.91
6%	2.93	1.60	1.01	1.88
7%	2.88	1.59	1.01	1.86
8%	2.84	1.58	1.00	1.84
rate of loan	2.0%	1.8%	1.6%	1.82%

The loans being shorter term, prepayments have a lower effect and duration of the stock is low. The "Noria" effect occurs fast.

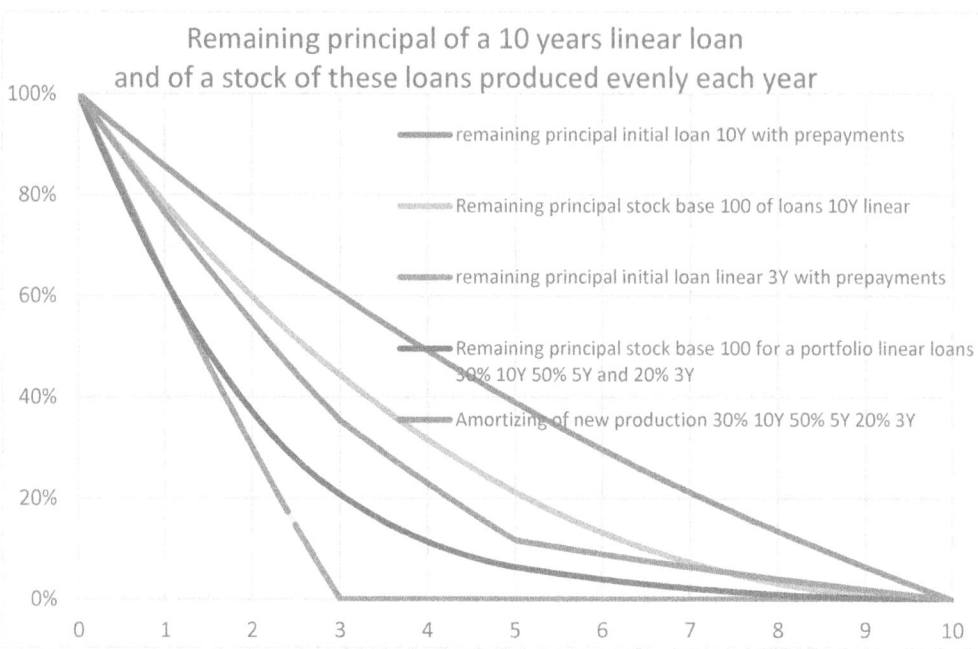

Let us assume that the final portfolio of the bank is made of 75% of mortgages loans (the ones with constant monthly payments) and 25% of equipment loans (the ones with linear amortization).

	weight	amount
mortgages	75%	45,000
linear	25%	15,000
Total	**100%**	**60,000**

The bank is indeed enjoying a significant mortgage portfolio representing 50% of its loans book. Still the total duration of the fixed rates loans portfolio (made of mortgages plus equipment loans) appears low:

CPR	total portfolio
3%	4.2
4%	4.1
5%	**4.0**
6%	3.9
7%	3.8
8%	3.7

<u>This is a key point. Even for banks producing 100% of mortgage loans, it is relatively rare to observe durations after prepayments above 5 years. This can happen in a configuration where there is low interest rates (but not decreasing because then prepayments soar) and aggressive very long-term new production, which unbalances the average duration of the stock because of these additional long duration recent loans.</u>

It means also that in our example, the "Noria" effect will occur fast, with 20% of the fixed rate portfolio amortizing in year one – that is 12 000 - as the graph of stock amortization shows:

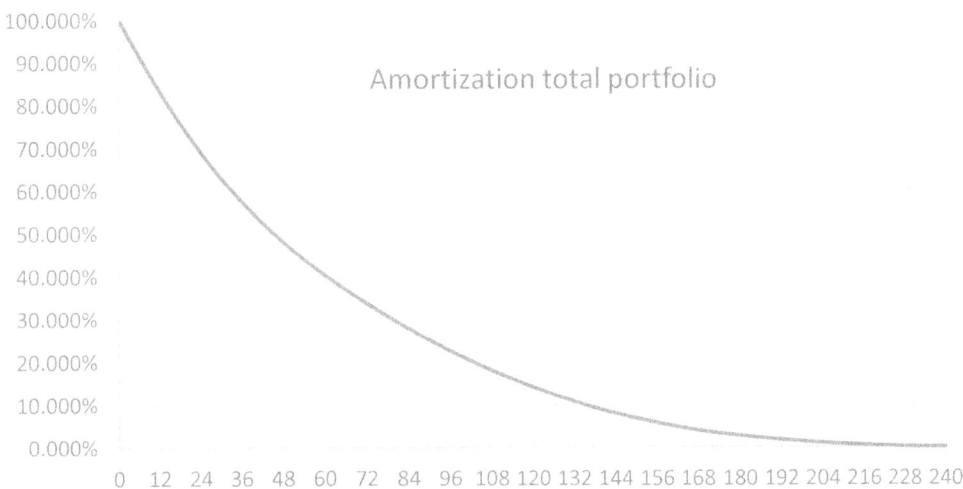

The first analysis that we made on the short-term exposure of the bank to IR has indeed improved: the "Noria" effect should take place fast enough so that the bank would take quickly advantage of increasing IR (and inversely would be quickly affected if IR were going down). In our example, the time lag effect that we mentioned will remain minimal. This is key because it means that the ALM managers must focus solely on their main exposure which is a decrease in the IR. It is the case in most of the banks that we have observed over the past few years.

Finally, notice that in the first approach, it is extremely reasonable to model the loans book using a simple exponential amortization curve. Many institutions make the mistake of refusing these fully justified approximations and go into time consuming processes of recalculating the amortization profile of each loan. This is most of the time useless and counter-productive since it slows the simulation in such a way that the ALM manager can not focus on their mission, which is mastering the key risks of the bank and testing their assumptions.

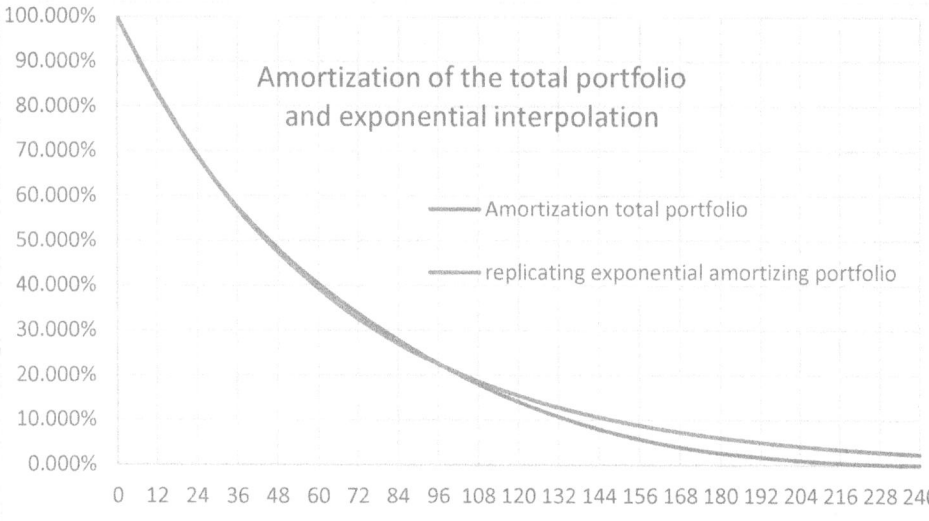

In our simulation, we use a similar approach but which may satisfy the ones concerned with the exactitude of the amortization profile of the stock: we calculate the exact profile for the fixed rate loans and then summarize them in one line. A better approach would be to have one line per vintage and type of loan because defaults and prepayments may differ, but this is not key for this paper focusing on the IRRBB.

For rolling the fixed rates loan into a new production, an elegant way is also to summarize in one line the profile of the resulting new production since this profile obviously differs from the stock (it is less convex). By doing so, we are precise on where we need to be, that is the 10 next years (and the following years, the error remains negligible), except that we do not distinguish prepayment behavior between subcategories.

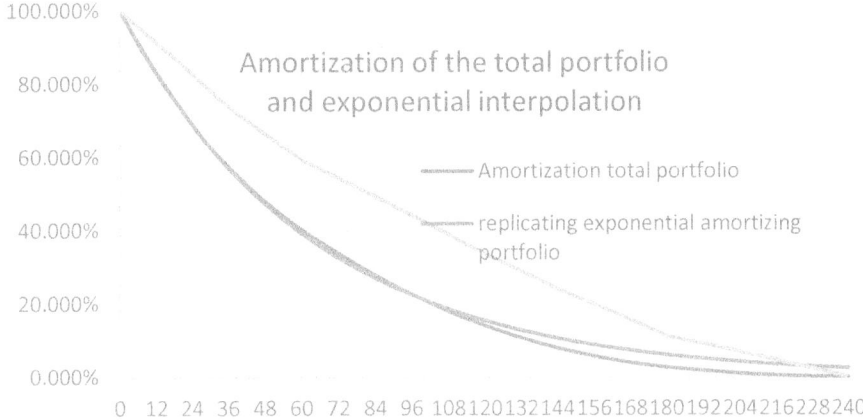

Liabilities: focusing on the Non Maturity Deposits ("NMD")

The liabilities of the bank appear also extremely classical with time deposits, issuances, current accounts and savings accounts. Time deposits and issuance are dated, so they can be modeled in a standard way (with prepayments). The two last categories have no maturity and in static gap, the regulator allows the institution to choose the conventional profile of targeted reinvestment[45] as long as the average duration of the total remains below the following limits:

---

[45] See "financial modeling of a commercial bank", ALM-Vision.

IRRBB d368 page 26 115. Banks should determine an appropriate cash flow slotting procedure for each category of core deposit, up to the maximum average maturity per category as specified in Table 2.

Table 2. Caps on core deposits and average maturity by category		
	Cap on proportion of core deposits (%)	Cap on average maturity of core deposits (years)
Retail/transactional	90	5
Retail/non-transactional	70	4.5
Wholesale	50	4

There is a degree of interpretation in the term "average duration". Indeed, duration can be considered as the modified duration, that is after taking into account or not the actualization factors. This will have to be clarified by regulators, since it has a significant impact on results.

Still in our example, whatever the definition, the average duration of the loans book remains below the cap of 5 years.

CPR	modified duration	average duration
3%	4.2	5.1
4%	4.1	4.9
5%	4.0	4.8
6%	3.9	4.6
7%	3.8	4.5
8%	3.7	4.4

The additional element to take into account is the fact that the limit in average maturity applies to "core deposits":

112. page 26 d368 "Banks should distinguish between the stable and the non-stable parts of each NMD category using observed volume changes over the past 10 years. The stable NMD portion is the portion that is found to remain undrawn with a high degree of likelihood. Core deposits are the proportion of stable NMDs which are unlikely to reprice even under significant changes in the interest rate environment. The remainder constitutes non-core NMDs…

114…. Non-core deposits should be considered as overnight deposits and accordingly should be placed into the shortest/overnight time bucket or time bucket midpoint."

Core deposits are actually extremely stable and well known in most countries since they constitute M1, the monetary mass and one of the key indicator of the central banks. M1 is directly linked to inflation, usually over-performing it by 2 to 4 points, which depends on:

- Interest rates: when IR are low, people leave their savings in their current accounts. When IR increase, they start to arbitrate and seek better protection against inflation by transferring into their savings accounts or by investing into time deposits. Most of the time, this phenomenon does not lead M1 to decrease but to increase at a slower rate, yet at a rate that is usually faster than inflation. Indeed, core deposits are extremely stable assets.
- Cyclicality: the cyclicality of core deposits varies according to key events of the year – end of summer vacation, end of year, tax period… Even depending on the days of shopping and vacation. These phenomena are also well mastered.

To summarize the new regulation, NMD ("No Maturity Deposits") should be split between:

- Non-stable: the part of the stock that varies,
- Stable: the stable part of the stock, that will be again split between the part of the stock that is:
    - Sensitive to IR: the part which may disappear in case of increase in IR or which pays a coupon sensitive to the variation of the IR,
    - Insensitive to IR: this constitutes the "core deposits"

<u>The non-core deposits are the sum of the non-stable deposits and those stable deposit that are sensitive to IR</u>.

For our example, we have translated the fact that the IR paid on savings accounts is an average of the Euribor over the last 6 months by assuming 10% of real core deposits, that is a target duration of reinvestment below 6 months. We also consider cyclicality to impact 5% of our stock which means that in total, our core deposit will be seen as over-night for a massive amount:

	Amount	Non stable		Stable sensitive		Real Core deposit		Cap on core (%)	Benchmark Total		Max. Duration	
		%	amount	%	Amount	%	Amount		JJ	Long term	For long term core	For deposit
Retail/transactional (current retail)	25,000	5	1,250	5	1,250	90	22,500	90	2,500	22,500	5	4.
Retail/non-transactional (savings)	20,000	10	2,000	80	16,000	10	2,000	70	18,000	2,000	4.5	0.4
Wholesale (current)	5,000	10	500	10	500	80	4,000	50(reached)	2,500	2,500	4	
Total current and savings	50,000	7.5	3,750	35.5	17,750	57.0	28,500		23,000	27,000	4.87	2.6

The regulation is restrictive with 46% of the current and savings accounts considered as Overnight from an IR point of view. That means that the maximum duration is 2.6 years for the sum of savings and currents accounts, this appears low.

However, we still have 54% of the NMD available for very long term funding since their maximum duration is 4.9 years. That means that the regulator allows us to use these 54% of NMD to refund our fixed rate portfolio. It means also that <u>we have an IR indicator of our target long-term issuance: this shall be around the difference between our long-term loans portfolio and our core deposits</u>. This is important since many banks have a tendency to refund themselves too short. Furthermore, this strategy minimizes the flattening risk between short-term and long-term interest rates.

The regulator provides some degrees of freedom for IR paying savings accounts. Indeed, many savings accounts do not have a direct sensitivity to IR. For example, some pay a formula equal to inflation plus a spread. Since inflation is not correlated at 100% with IR but rather between 50% and 70%, this is another grey area: the regulation qualifies as NMD any product which has no legal expiry date, whether it bears interest or not and whether this interest is correlated to the market or not. The criteria for considering an interest bearing stable deposit as core is that it is "unlikely to reprice" under the described scenarios. In the case of inflation paying savings, if the correlation is of 70%, it would be logical to consider 30% of these accounts as core.

In our example, we have a very interesting situation: savings account shall not reprice in the scenario where short term interest rates are going down and shall reprice in the opposite scenario where short term rates are going up. Indeed, the convention for amortization should depend on the scenario. <u>This is not mentioned in the regulation nor is it mentioned that we cannot change the convention of amortization per scenario</u>. We choose to take the less advantageous convention to the bank that is the shortest, which is the normal case. But by doing so, we massively underestimate our exposure to IR decrease in static gap, a very classical mistake.

Globally, from the point of view of static gap, the methodology of the regulator conducts to leads to the conclusion that the value of the stock of the bank will go down if IR are increasing: here, the implied duration of the capital would be of 10 years and a move of 200 bps would reduce its theoretical "IRRBB value" by around 20.6%, so out of the limits. This is counter-intuitive since the bank's NIM appears exposed to a decrease in IR.

	amount	duration		amount	duration
loan book	90,000	3.17	current and savings	50,000	2.63
treasury	8,000	0	short term deposit	20,000	0.25
Total assets	98,000	2.91	issuances	20,000	2.3
			total liabilities out of capital	90,000	2.03
			Fixed assets	-2,000	
			capital	*10,000*	*10.31*

If we assume that we can use the modified duration, things are slightly better but the antagonist conclusion does not change: the static gap still shows an exposure to the increase of the IR but this one remain inside the limits with the theoretical value of the "IRRBB capital" going down by only -11% when IR are up 2%.

	amount	duration		amount	duration
loan book	90,000	2.66	current and savings	50,000	2.63
treasury	8,000	0	short term deposit	20,000	0.25
Total assets	98,000	2.44	issuances	20,000	2.3
			total liabilities out of capital	90,000	2.03
			immo.	-2,000	
			capital	10,000	5.65

<u>Using the convention required by the regulator leads to underestimating the exposure of the bank to a decrease in IR. It can even lead to the opposite conclusion that a decrease in IR should increase the value of the stock of the bank.</u>

Actually, <u>the difference in duration between the stock of assets and the liabilities using regulatory conventions for NMD gives rather an idea of the position of the bank versus its benchmark of reinvestment of its NMD, after taking into account all the other dated positions.</u> It does not express the true exposure of the bank to IR.

However, we see that for our example using modified duration, the bank presents an acceptable exposure to IR and does not have to change its lending strategy. Is this conclusion an accurate translation of the reality? Why did the regulator choose such a position and how do we reconcile it with our first analysis? What is the optimum choice of duration for core NMD? To better understand this rules, we will first analyze the realty of the impact of an IR move on the income statement of the bank and subsequently on its market value.

NIM simulation and effect of IR on the value of the bank

We model the bank using ALM-Solutions® software, which allows exact replication of the income statement and balance sheet.

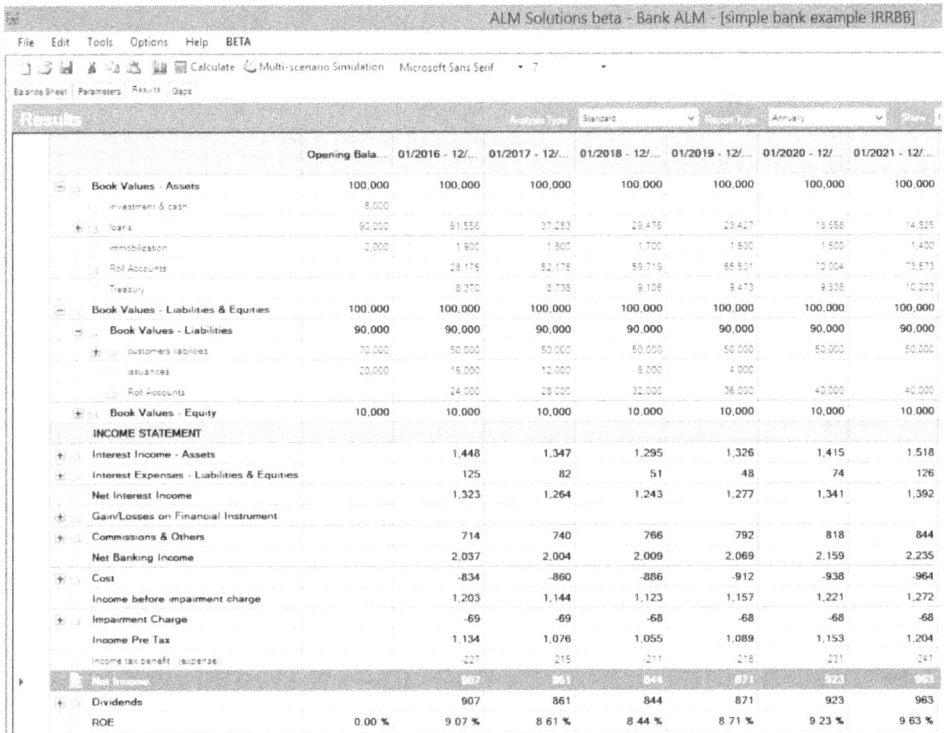

The ALM-Solutions® software replicates both the income statement and the balance sheet applying each accounting rule and adjusting the treasury accordingly. We do the calculation on 10 scenarios:

- Realization of the forward rates and translation of this realization by +1% and -1%
- We keep the curve flat and then translate it by +/- 1%
- We run the 6 regulatory stress test scenarios defined by IRRBB368

Prepayments are modified in translation scenarios: if IR are up by 1%, they go down 20% being 80% of the initial 5%. Inversely, if IR are down by 1%, they go up by 20% being 120% of the initial 5%.

The stock is "rolled" into a new production with identical characteristics.

Obviously, simulations confirm our first qualitative analysis: the bank is significantly exposed to a decrease in IR. Inversely, an increase in IR is favorable to the NIM even the first year. This is a very classical result and most retail banks have the same exposure even though our example shows a high sensitivity to IR.

Net Interest Income (NII) per scenario in dynamic gap

	Opening Bala.	01/2016 - 12/..	01/2017 - 12/..	01/2018 - 12/..	01/2019 - 12/..	01/2020 - 12/..	01/2021 - 12/..	01/2022 - 12/..
Book Values - Assets	100,000	100,000	100,000	100,000	100,000	100,000	100,000	100,001
investment & cash	8,000							
loans	90,000	61,956	37,263	29,476	23,427	18,658	14,825	11,801
immobilization	2,000	1,900	1,800	1,700	1,600	1,500	1,400	1,300
Roll Accounts		28,175	52,178	59,719	65,501	70,004	73,573	76,533
Treasury		8,370	8,758	9,106	9,473	9,830	10,203	10,567
Book Values - Liabilities & Equities	100,000	100,000	100,000	100,000	100,000	100,000	100,000	100,001

Scenario Comparison

Report Type: Annually   Show: Final

Scenario	01/2016 - 12/2016	01/2017 - 12/2017	01/2018 - 12/2018	01/2019 - 12/2019	01/2020 - 12/2020	01/2021 - 12/2021	01/2022 - 12/2022	01/20...
INCOME STATEMENT								
forward	1,322.96	1,264.29	1,243.4	1,277.16	1,341.23	1,391.63	1,404.49	
forward-1pct	1,082.11	1,040.94	970.88	879.54	1,033.28	1,068.39	1,073.19	
forward+1pct	1,470.72	1,390.92	1,416.69	1,458.81	1,496.37	1,520.02	1,552.09	
flat	1,319.97	1,229.47	1,157.01	1,109.47	1,079.96	1,049.77	1,004.95	
flat+1pct	1,466.38	1,345.1	1,320.6	1,300.03	1,281.6	1,267.85	1,255.77	
flat-1pct	1,078.97	1,005.06	982.15	807.4	768.05	722.89	646.56	
Reg_parallel_up	1,518.61	1,355.09	1,377.45	1,384.07	1,377.85	1,381.66	1,402.38	
Reg_parallel_down	879.7	789.04	628.33	521.62	474.78	415.67	307.19	
Reg_flattener	1,374.89	1,066.37	985.2	879.84	829.96	784.13	722.4	
Reg_steepener	1,057.39	1,162.56	1,127.76	1,107.53	1,098.53	1,084.41	1,057.12	
Reg_shortdown	842.16	958.9	877.21	831.3	812.43	784.44	729.18	
Reg_shortup	1,428.77	1,295.71	1,030.92	981.19	941.08	909.04	875.26	
Net Interest Income	1,322	1,264	1,243	1,277	1,341	1,392	1,404	

A CFO concerned with the volatility of his result would be eager to lend longer or to hedge, if swaps are available, by entering receiving swaps. By doing so, the CFO would be limited by the result of the static analysis we made, using regulatory conventions.

Obviously, if interest rates are going up, not only will the NIM of the bank increase but also subsequently its market value. Indeed, banks structurally are highly leveraged entities (requiring only about 10 to 15 of capital to manage a balance sheet of 100 or more) and their PER does not move that much with IR. Subsequently, every increase of the NIM directly affects their market value in proportion to their PER x (1-tax rate).

Our example is modeled as a complete bank, generating commissions, paying charges and cost of risk, plus taxes. The net income is supposed to be fully distributed. The bank appears in good standing except for its exposure to IR:

- Income around 1,000 that is almost 10% of ROE (Return on Equity) in the current context of extremely low IR,
- Cost/income ratio around 40%,
- Cost of risk pretty low at -69,
- Good balance between NIM and commissions.

Balance sheet and Income statement, « forward » scenario of realization of the forward

	Opening Bala...	01/2016 - 12/...	01/2017 - 12/...	01/2018 - 12/...	01/2019 - 12/...	01/2020 - 12/...
Book Values - Assets	100,000	100,000	100,000	100,000	100,000	100,000
Book Values - Liabilities & Equities	100,000	100,000	100,000	100,000	100,000	100,000
INCOME STATEMENT						
Interest Income - Assets		1,448	1,347	1,295	1,326	1,415
investment & cash		11				
loans		1,342	983	738	585	465
immobilization						
Roll Accounts		119	364	557	741	950
Treasury						
Interest Expenses - Liabilities & Equities		125	82	51	48	74
Interest Expenses - Liabilities		125	82	51	48	74
customers liabilities		-10	-10	-10	-10	-10
advances		185	145	105	65	25
Roll Accounts		-50	-73	-54	-27	39
Interest Expenses - Equity						
Net Interest Income		1,323	1,264	1,243	1,277	1,341
Gain/Losses on Financial Instrument						
Commissions & Others		714	740	766	792	818
Net Banking Income		2,037	2,004	2,009	2,069	2,159
Cost		-834	-860	-886	-912	-938
Income before impairment charge		1,203	1,144	1,123	1,157	1,221
Impairment Charge		-69	-69	-68	-68	-68
Income Pre Tax		1,134	1,076	1,055	1,089	1,153
Income tax benefit /(expense)		-227	-215	-211	-218	-231
Net Income		**907**	**861**	**844**	**871**	**923**
Dividends		907	861	844	871	923
ROE	0.00 %	9.07 %	8.61 %	8.44 %	8.71 %	9.23 %

The valuation of the bank is done using two methodologies:

- PER: 10 times the income in year 1

- Dividend Discount Model (DDM): actualized value of the income over 10 years at 10% plus final value of capital at 10%

Each methodology shows that the value of the bank decrease when interest rates decrease. It is interesting to notice that the PER even provides a sensitivity of the value of a bank to IR which is logically long term.

Note also that a decrease in interest rates effectively reduces the ROE of banks as it does for the rest of the economy: indeed, ROE are usually measured using a risk premium above the long term IR. Therefore, a decrease in this ROE when IR are decreasing is a normal phenomenon in the economic cycle. What matters is to keep it under control and to makes sure that the exposure is not excessive, since most of the banking costs are fixed: branches, employees, systems...

Income after taxes

	1	2	3	4	5	6	7	Market capitalisation	
Scenario	year 1	year 2	year 3	year 4	year 5	year 6	year 7	PER	DDM
forward	907.3	860.6	844.1	871.3	922.8	963.3	973.8	9,073	9,409
forward-1pct	714.6	681.9	626.0	632.4	676.4	704.7	708.8	7,146	8,038
forward+1pct	1,025.5	961.9	982.7	1,016.6	1,046.9	1,066.0	1,091.9	10,255	10,199
flat	904.9	832.7	774.9	737.1	713.7	689.8	654.2	9,049	8,388
flat+1pct	1,022.0	925.2	905.8	889.6	875.0	864.3	854.8	10,220	9,378
flat-1pct	712.1	653.2	555.1	495.5	464.2	428.3	367.4	7,121	6,876
Reg_parallel_up	1,063.79	933.19	951.3	956.81	952.04	955.3	972.58	10,638	9,861
Reg_parallel_down	520.68	480.35	345.6	266.85	229.59	182.51	95.94	5,207	5,431
Reg_flattener	948.8	702.62	613.49	553.42	513.73	477.28	428.11	9,488	7,401
Reg_steepener	694.82	779.17	751.55	735.58	728.59	717.5	695.89	6,948	8,260
Reg_shortdown	523.42	616.24	551.1	514.59	499.71	477.53	433.53	5,234	6,884
Reg_shortup	991.92	725.68	674.07	634.5	602.62	577.21	550.4	9,919	7,928

Each scenario would deserve a comment. Globally, we see that:

- The bank is exposed to a decrease in interest rates

- In the forward scenario, the IR increases gradually allowing the income to improve after a difficult period. In the flat scenario, the old loan portfolio made with higher IR is progressively amortizing and the loans are replaced with new loans at the current low market conditions. Subsequently, the income decrease progressively.
- The regulatory scenario of a decrease in interest rates (parallel shift down) assumes that IR is down by 2%: of course, with a 7 years swap at zero currently, it means loans at negative rate. This is absurd and actually regulators are allowed to keep IR positive or above a certain threshold. We have decided to keep the scenario as it is because (1) we have seen that it is not the scenario generating an issue in static gap and (2) in the current environment we still do not know which regulatory down scenario the regulator will recommend (having 10 years rate at -1.8% with commercial margin below 1% is generating a loss for each new loan!)

Subsequently, there is an antagonism between the requirement of the regulator expressed by the limits given in term of variation of value of the stock using its convention for valuing the NMD and the natural exposure of banks to a decrease in interest rates. This is a fundamental result of ALM and one of the danger of the application of the static gap analysis as a standalone methodology.

This different and even sometimes opposite view of risk is structural in nature. For most institutions, simulations show clear and significant exposure to IR decrease, as our qualitative analysis previously showed. These institutions are not obvious risk-takers: they simply serve their customers as they have done for years without any issue and for many they never faced any major issue, even during the 2008 crisis.

Still the regulator is eager to limit the transformation of NMD into long-term investment.

The reason of the structural difference between the two approaches is actually very logical and fully justified.

The static gap methodology is translating the concern of the regulator in case of liquidation.

The regulator is well aware of the dangers of the static gap methodology: it is clearly mentioned in the regulation:

§11 page 3 " *If a bank solely minimizes its economic value risk by matching the repricing of its assets with liabilities beyond the short term, it could run the risk of earnings volatility*".

It is a soft way of saying that the bank may take the wrong hedging position or move its business toward too much variable rates loans in front of much less sensitive liabilities.

This approach is by the way in the continuity of the regulation of July 2004, BCBS108, which already mentioned page 28 annex 1 point 7:

7. "*Although gap analysis is a very commonly used approach to assessing interest rate risk exposure, it has a number of shortcomings...*"

It also already emphasized the importance of a dual approach: "*simple maturity/repricing schedules can be used to generate simple indicators of the interest rate risk sensitivity of both earnings and economic value to changing interest rates*" (page 27. §4).

However, the regulator acknowledges that it is still favoring the static gap methodology:

11. "*While the economic value and earnings-based measures share certain commonalities, the Committee observes that most commercial banks primarily utilize the latter for IRRBB management, whereas regulators tend to endorse the former as a benchmark for comparability and capital adequacy.*" (page 3. D368)

The reason is very simple and actually is more related to capital adequacy than benchmarking (which can be done using the d368 conventions on NIM calculations): The concern of the regulator is different. It is more focused on its own risk <u>in case it has to liquidate the bank</u>. This approach justifies looking only at the stock and not to consider any new business since for the intervening regulator, there will be none. Obviously, if all lines were at variable rate, the liquidation would not face the risk of a variation of the Marked to Market (MTM) of the positions if IR were moving.

In this view, the regulator's main concern is the "No Maturity Deposits" (NMD) because in case of liquidation, it may have to give them back at par. Therefore, it would bear no risk if they were considered as overnight deposit[46]. Obviously banks strongly disagree with this view on their most valuable asset in most cases and de facto a very long-term and stable resource.

Indeed, the actual rule is simply a compromise between:

- The regulator who considers that NMD are a risk for the bank in case of liquidation and should not be used to refund excessively long-term IR exposure[47].
- The banks who consider that NMD have a MtM price which is highly sensitive to IR since it is a perpetual resource at 0 for most of the current accounts (or inversely with no sensitivity for savings account paying an IR highly correlated to the market short-term rate).

As we have seen, the compromise appeared as reasonable, since the duration of a loan book of a standard retail bank is below 5 years. However, as always, "the devil is in the details" and the margin of safety included in the regulation considering what is "core" and not "core" makes the constraints much more significant.

Seen from a dynamic gap point of view, a bank benefits from reinvesting its non interest-bearing NMD in long-term IR instruments in order to stabilize

---

[46] We do not take into account the fact some countries as in Europe have guarantee funds for deposits up to a certain amount.
[47] We are not speaking about liquidity which is handled separately but about IR exposure only.

its NIM, whereas the regulator wants to limit this transformation and have the banks invest them shorter term in order to avoid any excessive risk of MtM variation, even though it may result in a more volatile NIM.

So <u>the truce remains in a reasonable balance between excessive long-term transformation</u> (nobody would agree to reinvest current accounts at 30Y rates and face the risk of seeing a major change during this period to the activity of the bank or the economy) <u>and excessive short-term position</u> (symmetrically, investing its current accounts at overnight rate would not only be counterproductive but extremely risky for the bank).

Actually, both visions are not truly antagonist since, as in our example, <u>it is not in the interest of the regulator to force the bank to increase its exposure to a decrease in IR because this would result in a higher probability of default</u>.

Banks' ALM objective is to stabilize the NIM under the constraint of respecting the limits on variation in EVE.

From our previous discussion, it is clear that ALM managers will have to integrate this new requirement to their approach.

In the current regulation, banks can choose their parameters in term of duration of NMD and more importantly in term of percentage considered as core. In addition, they apply the same methodology to their capital which is not considered as a short-term resource either. Subsequently, the normal structure allows for the alignment of both risks – static and dynamic - showing a duration of liabilities above the duration of the assets.

It may no longer be the case in the new regulation after January 2018 and the objective of an ALM manager differs:

<u>The mathematical expression of the objective of ALM under IRRBB d368 will be to minimize the volatility of the NIM under the constraint of respecting regulatory limits in terms of variation of EVE</u>.

This raises the issue of knowing what to do if, as in our example, the application of d368 results in greater bank exposure to a decrease in interest rates.

Obviously, there are many cases where this would be fully justified and one understands perfectly that the benchmark of reinvestment of the NMD should remain reasonable. However, the new rule may have more impact. Indeed, imagine a book having mostly long-term mortgages, it is difficult to admit that this retail bank simply serving its retail and SME customers may have to face the paradoxical constraint of having to reduce its mortgage lending or enter into paying swaps in order to comply with IRRBB d368 (and pay the spread if the curve is "in contengo" that is IR increasing with duration). Obviously, nobody would do so. The most likely situation will be for the bank to issue longer-term covered bonds in order to adjust its liabilities.

<u>IRRBB d368 will push banks to improve their balance sheet management approach by having a more global view on their strategy of refunding</u>. This is a massive change with the previous clearly segregated approaches between liquidity and IR risks.

In our example, you may have noticed that the bank chose to refund itself with fixed rates issuances and not variable rates. There is a reason: by doing so, even though the bank increases its exposure to a downward translation of the IR curve, it reduces its risk of flattening or worse, of crisis on the short-term IR. This is where the new regulation may result in a much more sophisticated approach.

Calculating the EVE

For calculating the Economic Value of Equity, we shall use the methodology recommended in our previous memorandum on IRRBB368[48]: we simply price MtM each lines of the balance sheet using the amortizing rules resulting from the application of the conventions for NMD (note that the

---

[48] « The new standard for IRRBB defined by the Basel Committee on Banking Supervision: finally, ALM makes its revolution », July 2016. *Serge Moulin*. ALM-Vision research.

shift of the curve needs in this case to be taken initially and not the day after).

There are several advantages in this methodology: results are exact and we do not have to distinguish variable rates, spread, fixed rates... Indeed, we have a better estimate with a more flexible methodology. Notice that this methodology allows us to automatically get the value of the caps and floors and other derivatives as soon as these are properly input into to system.

Amortizing on the balance sheet in "static regulatory gaps" – "flat" scenario

	Opening Bala...	01/2016 - 12/...	01/2017 - 12/...	01/2018 - 12/...	01/2019 - 12/...	01/2020 - 12/...	01/2021 - 12/...	01/2022 - 12/...	01/2023 - 12/...
Book Values - Assets	100,000	63,622	39,233	31,353	25,215	20,346	16,404	13,064	10,269
investment & cash	8,000								
loans	90,000	61,722	37,433	29,853	23,615	18,346	15,004	11,764	9,069
fixed rate	60,000	47,455	37,433	29,853	23,615	18,346	15,004	11,764	9,069
variable rate	30,000	14,267							
immobilization	2,000	1,900	1,800	1,700	1,600	1,500	1,400	1,300	1,200
Roll Accounts									
Treasury									
Cash Adj									
Book Values - Liabilities & Equities	100,000	63,622	39,233	31,353	25,215	20,346	16,404	13,064	10,269
Book Values - Liabilities	90,000	63,622	39,233	31,353	25,215	20,346	16,404	13,064	10,269
customers liabilities	70,000	22,452	18,620	15,508	12,965	10,895	9,120	7,518	6,093
current accounts	30,000	22,452	18,620	15,508	12,965	10,895	9,120	7,518	6,093
savings accounts	20,000								
times deposits	20,000								
issuances	20,000	16,000	12,000	8,000	4,000				
Cash Adj									
Treasury		25,170	8,613	7,845	8,230	9,451	7,284	5,546	4,176
Roll Accounts									
Book Values - Equity	10,000								
capital		10,000							
INCOME STATEMENT									
Interest Income - Assets		1,336	992	741	589	469	375	296	231
investment & cash		-11							
loans		1,347	992	741	589	469	375	296	231
fixed rate		1,139	929	741	589	469	375	296	231
variable rate		155	53						
immobilization									
Roll Accounts									
Treasury									
Cash Adj									
Interest Received On Derivatives									
Interest Expenses - Liabilities & Equities		167	145	105	65	25			
Interest Expenses - Liabilities		167	145	105	65	25			
customers liabilities		-18							
current accounts									
savings accounts		3							

The equity appears as an overnight liability in order to keep its MTM equal to the nominal, whatever the scenario.
In order to neutralize the creation of income, we assume a full distribution.

Obviously, the amortizing of the balance sheet will depend on the scenarios due to the different prepayment speed (the treasury effect is annulated since all income are paid as dividend).

Scenario	Opening Balance	01/2016 - 12/2016	01/2017 - 12/2017	01/2018 - 12/2018	01/2019 - 12/2019	01/2020 - 12/2020	01/2021 - 12/2021
flat	100.000	63.621.68	53.672.72	47.789.69	42.405.5	37.391.11	35.615.59
Reg_parallel_up	100.000	64.244.34	54.081.66	48.213.33	42.845.69	37.848.41	36.072.89
Reg_parallel_down	100.000	63.004.73	53.199.38	47.302	41.901.81	36.871.05	35.095.53
Reg_flattener	100.000	63.004.73	53.945.7	48.048.32	42.643.13	37.617.37	35.841.85
Reg_steepener	100.000	64.244.34	53.342.52	47.474.19	42.106.55	37.109.27	35.333.75
Reg_shortdown	100.000	63.004.73	53.114.43	47.217.05	41.816.85	36.786.09	35.010.57
Reg_shortup	100.000	64.244.34	54.144.16	48.275.93	42.908.2	37.910.92	36.135.4

The IRRBB368 calculation simply require to value MTM all balance sheet and compare the results between stressed scenarios and the reference one. Notice that the valuation of the reference scenario does not need to use the correct market spread for valuating loans since we just focus on the variation (the effect is negligible compared to the IR effect). Notice also that our methodology has the advantage of using natively the proper IR curve to actualize each line and is an enhanced methodology compared to the one accepted by the regulator with wider time bucket and approximations in term of spread.

Scenario	Assets	customer deposits	issuances	total liabilities	EVE	Var. EVE
flat	105,741	69,932	20,643	90,576	15,166	0
Reg_parallel_up	101,035	67,546	19,616	87,161	13,874	-1,292
Reg_parallel_down	111,549	73,248	21,825	95,073	16,476	1,310
Reg_flattener	106,053	70,347	20,470	90,817	15,236	71
Reg_steepener	105,411	69,635	20,823	90,458	14,953	-213
Reg_shortdown	107,503	70,865	21,327	92,192	15,311	145
Reg_shortup	104,072	69,112	19,999	89,111	14,962	-204

The worst scenario is parallel up with a variation in EVE of 13% of the capital.

Without surprise, results confirm our qualitative analysis and duration analysis: the static gap methodology generates a constraint for banks, expressing the risk faced by a central bank on the stock in case of run-off if IR are going up. This depends obviously of the conventions on what is a core deposit. As we have seen, results are extremely sensitive to these conventions as well as the prepayment assumptions. Banks will have to be extremely cautious when defining both.

Notice that our example stays, as anticipated, inside its 15% limit of capital. However, this appears to be a pretty unstable result even though our example was made to show the danger of the static gap methodology since we chose a very disadvantageous modeling of the savings accounts as well as relatively low prepayment curve.

This modeling has a heavy consequence: we cannot hedge sufficiently against the main risk of the bank, that is a decrease of the IR whether by entering receiving swaps or by expanding our portfolio of fixed rates long-term loans. In this situation, the bank should naturally reconsider its assumptions in term of stability of deposits in order to gain some flexibility. But this will necessarily imply a negotiation with the regulator.

The gap buckets analysis

The bucket analysis is a useful complementary element of information on the IR position but cannot be used as the main element of decision, even though it is still the case in some banks.

The ALM-Solutions® software automatically computes the analysis allowing us to complete our case study. The curve shows a regular decrease of the exposure of a cyclical nature due to the fact that issuances are done quarterly. Only the first point appears as significantly unbalanced at 4.5 billion (bn.). This is the simple application of our conventions:

- In the assets: 8 bn. treasury plus 30 bn. variable rates loans and 0.8 bn. fixed rates loan amortization
- For liabilities: 3.5 bn. of conventional amortization of current accounts and 40 b. of savings and times deposits at variable rates.

After this "excess" of liabilities at very short-term, we see logically an excess of assets with a slight distortion coming from the issuances.

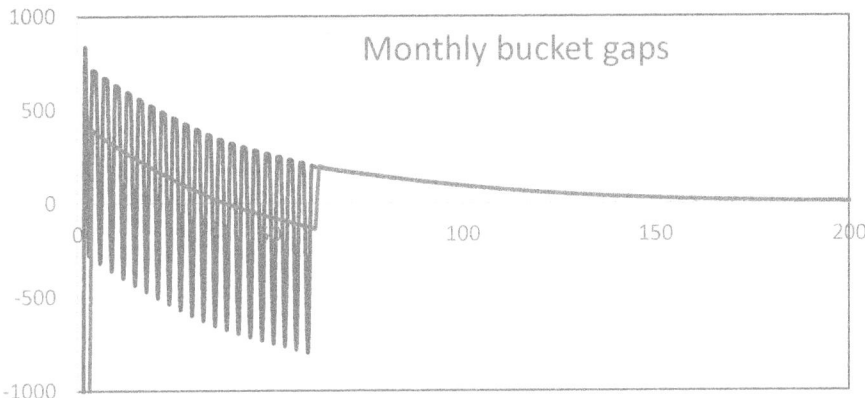

The "excess" of very short-term liabilities is an intrinsic characteristic of the banking industry which is based on the transformation of short-term deposits into longer term loans. This is perfectly normal and does not necessary express an excess in risk. A banking proverb says that "loans make deposits" to express the fundamental mechanism of monetary creation. Notice that the first bucket could show significantly different results, should the convention on savings or currents accounts be differed.

Optimizing the amortization profile of NMD

We choose a logical profile for amortizing our NMD that is to replicate the amortizing of our stock of fixed rates loan. Other shapes are possible, for example:

- Linear amortization: this simple shape is used by many banks
- Replicating the amortization of the portfolio for durations above 5 years and then adjusting before in order to respect the limit of 5 years duration. This shape was chosen without the 5 years duration constraint which is making it more complex and less attractive.

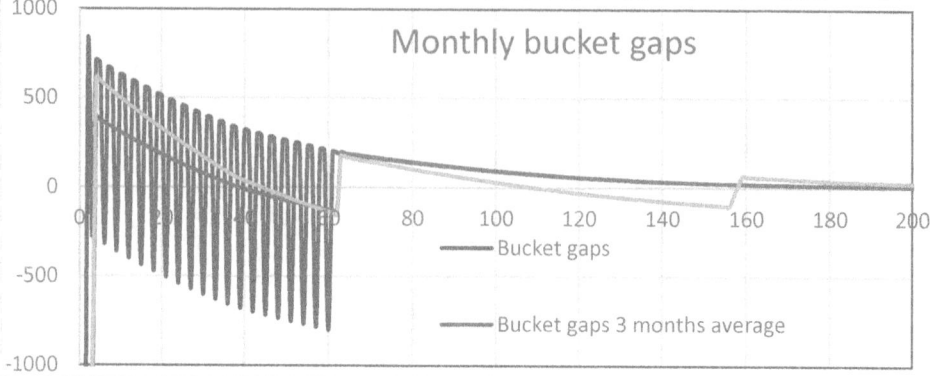

The graph shows that the linear convention generates a less regular profile especially in the long term. This may be a trap. Indeed, we have seen banks which decided to hedge the long term flattener the convention created by entering forward swaps. That is why it is recommended:

- to limit its hedging strategy to the first years: 3 to 5 years and then open its exposure
- to be reasonable and consistent, hedging for example every quarter up to 7 years swaps
- to always implement a multiple approach in analyzing its IR exposure.

Conclusion

IRRBB368 is a revolution in ALM. It requires a much more rigorous and technical approach than previously: modeling of dynamic gaps, definition of scenarios with variation of CPR, MtM valuation of the banking book... However, the limits imposed by the regulator to hedge the natural exposure to a decrease in interest rates of most banks may become an issue if regulators are not reasonable in their interpretation of the text. They should be reasonable since the first guarantee of a safe banking system is to have properly hedged banks, that generate regular income and are well prepared for difficult times when risk increases and, due to the subsequent recession, interest rates decrease.

From an operational point of view, too many banks are late in their preparation for implementing the new regulation both in terms of systems and more importantly and of concern, in terms of expertise in ALM.

Some qualitative macroeconomic and strategic perspectives on the current economic situation and what scenario we can imagine for 2017.

In 2012, we wrote that the worse scenario for financial institutions in the post crisis environment would be a Japanese crisis coming from the disappearance of growth in the Eurozone. We remain with the perspective that the main danger is an economy without growth. However we now see much more fundamental issues in the world economy: the beginning of the 21st century is faced with massive changes in demography, in meteorology, in economics and subsequently in geo-strategy. The world economy is undergoing a real mutation and we observe massive trade imbalance between Asia and most developed countries, as well as within the Eurozone, with consequent changes in economic models and governments struggling to restructure and adapt to the current fundamental evolution.

Changes generate uncertainty and risks and history shows that changes do not always occur in a progressive manner but rather through crisis and violent adjustments, amplifying the movements in the short -term. Investing will require more than ever clear strategic foresight, adaptability and nerves.

Fundamental macroeconomic issues remain in Europe

The secret virtues of devaluation disappeared in the Eurozone
The current market's heavy and silent nightmare of low interest rates without credit spread is the consequence of structural issues in the European economy that are killing growth: many countries, like Italy but also France to a lesser extent, used to compensate lax cost control which were pushing their competitiveness down by devaluation. By doing so, they were implementing a very smart strategy improving their competiveness internationally while controlling consumption of foreign goods internally.

And at the same time they were reducing the value of savings: the strategy was advantageous not only for the exporting industries but also for every working (and subsequently producing) people since they were able to compensate for inflation. This was to the disadvantage of retired people or any not actively producing people. Indeed, this passive policy was a very strong incentive for people to produce, to put their money at work by actively investing. It was an extremely powerful model of redistribution of wealth toward investment. It was also an incentive to create job inside the country since exporting industries knew that they would increase profit by simply trying to better control their costs than the average. Finally, by benefiting the population involved in the value creation, it was also benefiting its profile of consumption that is structurally more local. Indeed, the devaluation/inflation mechanism is extremely subtle and powerful. And last but not least, this mechanism was automatic and politicians did not have to be active.

The introduction of the EURO stopped this virtuous cycle by blocking the most fundamental way for many economies to adjust. But nobody was used to sing the benefits and virtue of devaluation and inflation, especially in front of electors, who are retired for a higher percentage than in the global population. No politicians either reacted by applying the German rigor in cost control and by pushing for quality improvement in order to compete with new actors in the global economy, with structural lower cost of labor (and no minimum wage which is currently a key element of the massive unemployment).

The International Monetary Fund (IMF) saw the issue when its Chief Economist, M. Blanchard, challenged the German taboo of a world with no inflation to suggest a more flexible inflation target of around 4%. Obviously, he did not argue about the forbidden virtues of inflation/devaluation but simply suggested that it would give more flexibility to the Central Bank to react in case of crisis.

Actually, this fundamental issue appeared gradually. The introduction of the EURO reduced quickly the cost of money at the beginning and many economies did not notice the issue, including the European Union which remained blind, focused on the political aspect of the union. It indeed forgot that the economy and political systems are intrinsically connected until the disequilibrium became obvious following the great financial crisis of 2008. The difficulty of the situation is that it appears rather cultural with countries performing well (former East European republics, Ireland) and others losing momentum (the south).

GDP per Capita	2000	2005	2008	2009	2010	2011	2012	2015	var. 15Y
Belgium	36,404	38,961	40,694	39,459	40,176	40,544	40,320	40,988	12.6%
France	34,119	35,711	36,801	35,536	36,057	36,626	36,513	36,928	8.2%
Germany	36,035	37,127	40,471	38,331	39,993	41,462	41,587	42,522	18.0%
Greece	24,387	29,021	31,301	29,876	28,203	25,665	23,920	23,575	-3.3%
Ireland	38,643	46,304	45,019	42,556	43,225	43,043	42,448	58,117	50.4%
Italy	35,400	36,297	36,517	34,320	34,752	34,818	33,680	33,156	-6.3%
Slovak Republic	15,479	19,850	25,108	23,694	24,833	25,684	26,070	28,095	81.5%
Spain	29,495	32,366	33,593	32,124	31,994	31,556	30,612	31,713	7.5%
Euro area (19 countries)	33,505	35,306	37,149	35,358	36,014	36,482	36,071	36,845	10.0%

Data extracted from OECD. Stat, US Dollar 2010, Gross domestic product (expenditure approach), per head, constant prices, constant PPPs.

The ECB is indirectly seeking to generate inflation to at least benefit the Eurozone against the rest of the world. But since its policy cannot differentiate between its members' countries, it cannot solve this internal fundamental issue.

Riccardo was also misinterpreted

An old businessman from Michigan told me one day that he was fine to compete with anybody on this earth as long as the rules were the same for all. Unfortunately, it is not the case and shortly after he sold his still flourishing company and retired, the buyers closed the main plant, destroying the first industry of the city and the work of his life. The decision was however logical and rational: they would produce at a cheaper cost in China. It was simply applying the principal of free trade: the market should readjust. Indeed it does. Population is leaving Michigan and its closing industry and the remaining people are gradually impoverished. For a time, credit helped them maintain their standard of living but in the end, this one will decrease to the advantage of the Chinese consumer who will replace them as output for the industry. Actually, this sounds logical and conforms to the free trade efficiency theory: the world as a whole is achieving a more efficient state... But it is also a rationale that the Michigan labor class disagrees with...

Indeed, Riccardo and Adam Smith showed both the virtue of free trade using two counties <u>competing with the same rules</u> (since they are both located in England). One is rural, wealthy with sheep and so can produce clothes in wool at a lower price with more flexibility whereas the other enjoys a good harbor and can import cotton and use it in a more efficient manner. Riccardo brilliantly argued that the two counties should specialize <u>and exchange</u> produce to achieve a higher global optimum, in what will be later seen as a Nash equilibrium. Just Adam Smith's reasoning does not apply to most of the classical industries in the USA and Europe: first these ones do not compete with the same rules as the emerging countries and, second, they do not benefit in the current competition the reciprocity of an exchange of goods and services between two economic actors.

The issue applies to many American states who surprised the media with their recent vote, it also applies to many European countries who are now entering a worse spiral: increase in poverty, degradation of education, asphyxia of the still alive industries which need carry some of the burden of unemployment (through an increase of their social charges and taxes...), worsening of the public debt... Indeed, the model of free exchange requires an exchange. That is an equivalent amount of services or good sold to the other partner (called a partner since you need to partner to get a better global optimum of wealth). Germany favors this model because the country is entering a real exchange economy. We observe the same with California or New York State (providing more service). These are mechanically in favor of free trade because they benefit from it. But for others, the model does not work and trade negotiation will inevitably become tougher, as the new American president started to state.

Within Europe, where the rules are relatively comparable, Adam Smith is not working better than between China and the state of Michigan: Germany increases its market share to the disadvantage of Italy, France and other countries that do not adapt to the new model. But inversely we observe that some countries are able to cope with it as in the North of Europe in

Hungary, Poland, Ireland... It seems that Adam Smith requires not only comparable rules but also a comparable business culture, something much more difficult to change. In addition, in Europe, the model of free trade implies that the workforce can move from one country to the other. This is a fundamental principle of the European Union. However, the principle does not solve the language and cultural barriers and Germany is not attracting significant free labor force from other European countries (which may explain their recent immigration strategy) which would reduce unemployment. Neither does Germany have incentive to invest in Italy.

The adaptation of the business culture in Europe in order to achieve a more balanced model is a long-term fundamental challenge and the European Union will have to seriously see how to support the countries in need of changes, unfortunately not simply with money but also with education and political communication. As of today, nothing significant is appearing in this direction and therefore, we can anticipate increased political turmoil in the south of Europe, including in France until decisions are inevitable.

The morphine of the Central Bank releases pain in the short-term but does not cure the disease.

The ECB is trying to help the weakest governments by easing their financial burden through the massive acquisition of their debt, without distinction of risk. This policy is equivalent to morphine injection: it does not cure the disease but anaesthetize the sick country: its government does not feel the pressure as strongly as before and, like in France, instead of taking the opportunity of this temporally relief to restructure, just leaves the situation in the same state, slowly continuing its deep damages to the economy. Like with morphine, the sick country gets accustomed to the debt purchase and just can not get out of the treatment, without imploding. It gradually asks for more in complete contradiction with the reassuring statements of the ECB which is entering the classical spiral of artificial support to its borrowers.

It rather transfers the misbalance into the balance sheet of the ECB which will have to take the loss at some point in time.

Obviously, this translates into its balance sheet which showed a very concerning growth these recent years. The model is even more dangerous that the disequilibrium in commercial balance inside Europe between Germany and the rest of the Eurozone just get translated into the balance sheet of the ECB: through the ECB, Germany is currently lending to its partners to fund their acquisitions of German goods... The model cannot last forever. At some point in time the ECB will have to bargain a massive and progressive write down of these public debts in exchange for fundamental reforms... A European soft version of an IMF intervention. The later the decision will be made, the more painful and violent it may be, the more complex the implementation.

Note that for a country, leaving the Eurozone would not be a more attractive future. The economy would automatically and instantly adjust. The currency would collapse, remaining industries would be in high difficulties on their input, and foreign investments would flight away.

The problem of Europe is to enter into gradual restructuring in order to smooth the pain and generate the growth that is the only hope out of the crisis.

The liquidity trap

The injection of liquidity by the ECB is not generating significant inflation of consumer prices. The mechanism of transmission of the growth of M1 to prices seems no longer to be working in a sufficiently powerful way to reactivate inflation. The same issue is observed in Japan.

Actually, the injections are generating one indirect inflationary phenomena: the inflation of the price of assets, or at least their artificial support. If the phenomena is not properly captured by CPI (cost of living includes a cost of housing but this does not directly express the variation of value of real estate), it may represent a time bombshell the day that the support will disappear.

Inversely, the liquidity injected by the ECB is actually frozen by the economic actors that use it to build reserves. But these massive reserves will have either to be destroyed or to be used at some point in time. The ECB assumes that the phenomena should take place gradually, with the recovery. But there are many scenarios where it could generate a massive deflagration: if at some point in time, a nation state considers leaving the euro or considers defaulting on its own debt, for example.

An excessive increase in Interest Rates would be suicidal for the ECB

With the US economy recovering and reaching again full employment, interest rates in the US are on the rise, which weakens the euro. If the devaluation of the EURO is positive for the economy, out of energy cost, the past reaction of the ECB has been to increase interest rates to avoid capital flow in a massively indebted economy. However, it would be a dangerous decision nowadays because of the size of some national public debts.

It is also impressive to observe that Europe hasn't really been able to take opportunity of the current growth in the USA: it gives a fair indicator of the current structural difficulties faced by Europe.

Figures are most of time shown in percentage of GDP. Rarely are they analyzed as they should be in percentage of revenues. Of course, it is supposed to be easy to increase revenues by increasing taxes, but this reduces activity as Laffer brilliantly expressed it. The best example is France which was not really able to fix its massive disequilibrium by increasing taxes. Unfortunately, what we observe is that the countries with the highest debt are also the ones with the highest deficit in percentage of revenues. If like Greece, France and Italy, the level of tax is already excessively high, the only solution is to reduce spending, add growth and in parallel write down part of the debt.

2015 (billions euro)	GDP	public revenues	public spending	excess / deficit	deficit in % revenues	public debt	debt in % of revenues	revenues in % of GDP	debt in % of GDP
EUROZONE	10413	4852	5061	-208	-4.3%	9440	195%	47%	91%
Belgium	410	210	221	-11	-5.1%	434	206%	51%	106%
Germany	3026	1350	1328	21	1.6%	2153	160%	45%	71%
Ireland	215	70	75	-5	-7.0%	201	286%	33%	94%
Greece	176	85	97	-13	-15.0%	311	368%	48%	177%
Spain	1081	413	468	-55	-13.4%	1072	260%	38%	99%
France	2190	1165	1244	-79	-6.8%	2097	180%	53%	96%
Italy	1636	784	826	-43	-5.4%	2172	277%	48%	133%
Netherland	679	292	305	-13	-4.4%	442	151%	43%	65%
Poland	1790	696	743	-47	-6.7%	918	132%	39%	51%
Portugal	179	79	87	-8	-10.0%	231	294%	44%	129%

Even these figures may misrepresent the level of deficit some countries run on their general budget (that is out of social security). In France, it is superior to 25% of the revenues (even though this includes some social transfer). Clearly, this is unsustainable on the long-term.

A new Keynesian support to consumption should be so inefficient that it may even aggravate the situation after a temporary artificial support

The current strategy to get out of the current negative spiral is based on the observation that the world global growth remains good at around 3% and should participate to the recovery. This one should be initiated by a classical strategy of budget or fiscal stimulus.

Actually, **a nation state like France has been under inefficient budget stimulus for 20 years**: indeed, growth (between 0 and 2% of GDP) is there below the budget deficit (between 2 and 4%, more during the crisis). Without this budget deficit, the French GDP growth would have been much lower if not negative (real estimate is difficult since the economy would have had to adapt and may have achieved better global result as this adaptation. Furthermore, this means that each time the state borrows one euro that it injects into the economy, a significant part of it evaporates out of France... It may sustain world growth but to the disadvantage of the country in the long-term. It is very different to sustain consumption, which has a high rate of loss for a national economy consuming also foreign goods, than to sustain innovation and investment inside the country, which generates revenues and employment. Furthermore, sustaining consumption doesn't allow leverage whereas adding capital through tax releases or supports to the corporates takes advantage of the structural leverage of the economy. The difference of efficiency of one euro injected into the economy is massive: between 6 to 10 times more efficient.

The model of the new deal of Roosevelt during the 30s is not working anymore because economies are much more international and currently are not sustained by the structural traditional double growth factor: a controlled population growth and increased education bringing innovation. If demography does not seem to be the current issue in a Europe crippled by unemployment and still enjoying a massive reserve of workflow, why isn't innovation more efficient currently?

Is innovation the saver of the current developed world crisis or does it increase it?

The usual model to solve the described misbalance, like for Germany or California, is to position the developed country on innovation and added value. The argument is self-understanding and has been powerful enough in the past to prove Marx wrong in its theory of the downward trend of the rate of margin. Both France and Italy have very dynamic technology sector. However, it seems insufficient. And definitely the topic is of concern to Spain, Portugal or Greece, three countries with a less powerful research sector. If innovation has always been the world growth vector (from the introduction of horses to plow, the wheel, coal...), its pace cannot be decided by governments, not even by pouring more money into research. Clearly money helps: it has been the long-term strategy of the USA to buy the best brains. But the USA's strategy is also to give them such an environment valuing innovation and creativity that they are incentivized to create and keep searching. Europe has to compete on this field with the USA and now China: indeed the new giant is producing more engineers and Ph.D. than any other country, including the USA since 2008.

Furthermore, Europe as a whole, is discovering that new technologies have **an effect of concentration of the added value, wealth and subsequently power** into a small hand of players: Google took over a massive share of the advertising business to national agencies, Amazon is the first shop in the world. Current innovation generates technical disruptions: some industries are being progressively replaced (taxis with Uber, advertising agencies...). The development of big data may increase the technological advantage of these world giants, who have been at the leading edge of the subject. For the world economy, this is a benefit since it needs less people, less work to perform a more efficient service. However, the phenomena is currently impressive by its amplitude and its social impact. Countries try to react to the threat that these platforms (Airbnb, Uber...) represent for their revenues (since they allow avoiding VAT and often taxes on revenues) but they still have to reposition part of their industry in fields that are less exposed to this massive economy of scale.

A multi-polar world is emerging with "Realpolitik" coming back challenging traditional political powers.

China is growing fast and with its economic growth comes the growth of its military power: the South China Sea crisis is a clear message that China will, as did the USA with the First World War, ask for the geostrategic dividends of its new economic strength. With 1800 warplanes against 3000 for the USA worldwide, its air force has already supremacy over the Sea of China (even more since its stealth submarines seem able to enter the safety zone around US carrier battle groups). The USA, feeling that its previously unchallenged supremacy is disappearing toward a new multipolar world and having a level of debt too high to maintain high military spending will have to review its strategy and focus on efficiency, which means that Europe will have also to review its defense policy and spending.

It is now clear that diplomacy between the different zones will become more complex and tense, considering the difficult economic situation. Previous systematic alignment to the USA received a serious blow to its prestige with the lies around the second Gulf war motivations. The Syrian crisis is showing that other more pragmatic strategies can be implemented more efficiently and with better results than what the USA did.

The world is rich in unstable areas: Turkey is becoming a focal point for competing stakeholders, the Middle East is destabilized by war, there is a power vacuum in Libya with two third of the population having fled the war and its massive energy reserve that are an attractive prey, Ukraine is economically severely challenged with unsolved conflict in the east ... The UN is challenged regularly and international law is not a better safeguard today than before.

In this complex situation, it is clear that Europe is not in running order: the European Commission is weakened and crippled by lobbying, national governments have difficulties to reach agreements and fundamental macroeconomic issues are not even clearly asserted.

A time of political instability marked by the rise of adventurers

The 20th century traditional parties are challenged everywhere and, with their power and credibility weakening, it is no surprise we observe the rise of new political formations and the appearance of political adventurers, who try to grab power that they see vacant or too weak to face the current environment. Obviously, these kinds of psychological profiles and competencies may be opportunities of regenerating the system but it may also be a dangerous hazard, increasing political instability.

In this environment, a crisis scenario can arise at any time in Europe

If we see more than ever, reasons for a real crisis inside the Eurozone with a massive widening of spreads, especially of govies and a jump in default rates, probability of such a scenario is difficult to estimate. However, considering the past pace of crisis, we can consider a probability of at least 25% for a major crisis in the next two years which is sufficient to justify preparing balance sheets to its occurrence. In this crisis, our most likely scenario would be a partial default on public debt. If it may be positive in the long run, it may generate a loss of confidence in the system, a repricing of other sovereign debts and overreactions. If the crisis is triggered by some international issue, it may spread to all the Eurozone, including to Germany.

Interest rates would automatically react by decreasing with the ECB keeping short-term rates at or below zero. Inflation would also collapse as well as the stock exchange. NPL are at historically low levels and would rise again whereas deposits would flee to safe havens: gold, real estate...

Therefore, it is more than ever the time to reconsider its assets in govies: many spreads are artificially maintained at low levels and do not translate the historical risk of sovereign default of some countries. Even though it appears to be easy money, the carry of such positions is nowadays a serious bet which has little to do with the economic business of most financial institutions.

About ALM-VISION

ALM-Vision is a quantitative modeling company founded in 2011. Its mission is to provide quantitative analysis and scientific support to financial institutions.

The core of our business activity is Asset Liability Management (ALM) modeling. Our modeling tool ALM-Solutions® is proprietary software developed internally by our team for highly precise state of the art modeling of banking assets and liabilities to monitor the financial institutions' interest rate, credit and liquidity risk and to understand the impact of a variety of economic scenarios on the balance sheet and income statements, including stress testing. We have also high quality pricing capacities for complex structured financial products.

In addition to ALM modeling, ALM-Vision provides advisory services to financial institutions and is called in to intervene on technical matters that require high pricing capacity and substantial and extensive experience in the financial markets (CVA, FVA, deal structuring, ABS, NBT, inflation-linked products, commodity derivatives and modeling, credit restructuring...).

Most bank ALM and/or risk teams are left alone to handle the new regulatory environment. With the current difficult environment for the financial industry, both human and technological resources are scarce and the teams have neither the time nor the capacity to develop the scientific part of their job. We provide our customers with this technical support and act as a bridge for best practices between our customers. Indeed, each customer brings us new needs, new issues, new requirements which reinforce our expertise. Our rule is to systematically share new non-client specific developments as a way to diffuse best practices around the industry. We strongly believe that our success is based on the fact that we aren't a simple IT provider but a true scientific support team, with strong financial expertise assisting our customers in the whole modeling and analysis of their balance sheet.

In ALM, software is just the tool. The core of the added value is the modeling and the analysis. Leveraging on our strong financial and market experience, we help our customers to focus on this core in the most efficient way.

Disclaimer

The contents of this document are proprietary to ALM-VISION. This document is produced by ALM-VISION for institutional investors only and is not financial research. This document is for information purposes only and is neither an offer to buy or sell, nor a solicitation or a recommendation to buy or sell, securities or any other product. ALM-VISION makes no representation as to the accounting, tax, regulatory or other treatment of the structure of any transaction and/or strategy described in this document and the recipient should perform its own investigation and analysis of the operations and the risk factors involved before determining whether such transaction is one which it is proper and appropriate for it to enter into. Some information contained in this document may have been received from third party or publicly available sources that we believe to be reliable. We have not verified any such information and assume no responsibility for the accuracy or completeness thereof. This document may also include details of historic performance levels of various rates, benchmarks or indices. Past performance is not indicative of future results.

© **2016 ALM-VISION.** www.alm-vision.com. **Contact** info@alm-vision.com. **All rights reserved. No information in this document may be reproduced or distributed in whole or in part without the express written prior consent of ALM-VISION, except for personal use.**

www.ingramcontent.com/pod-product-compliance
Lightning Source LLC
Chambersburg PA
CBHW060847170526
45158CB00001B/268